M Smith

D1480736

M Smith

STANDARD ENCYCLOPEDIA OF

Opalescent Glass

SECOND EDITION

IDENTIFICATION & VALUES

BILL EDWARDS

COLLECTOR BOOKS

A Division of Schroeder Publishing Co., Inc.

The current values of this book should be used only as a guide. They are not intended to set prices, which vary from one section of the country to another. Auction prices as well as dealer prices vary and are affected by condition as well as demand. Neither the Author nor the Publisher assumes responsibility for any losses that might be incurred as a result of consulting this guide.

Searching for a Publisher?

We are always looking for knowledgeable people considered to be experts within their fields. If you feel that there is a real need for a book on your collectible subject and have a large comprehensive collection, contact Collector Books.

On the Cover:

Top left: Singing Birds tumbler whimsey, blue opalescent, only one known, $1,500.00.
Bottom left: Dugan's Diamond Compass (Dragon Lady), $95.00.
Bottom right: Daisy and Drape vase, vaseline opalescent, rare, $1,500.00.

Cover design by Beth Summers
Book design by Mary Ann Dorris

Additional copies of this book may be ordered from:

Collector Books
P.O. Box 3009
Paducah, Kentucky 42002-3009

@$19.95. Add $2.00 for postage and handling.
Copyright: Bill Edwards, 1997

Inquiries (with SASE) may be sent to:
Bill Edwards
620 W. 2nd St.
Madison, IN 47250

This book or any part thereof may not be reproduced without the written consent of the Author and Publisher.

Dedication

For my good friends, Bob and Pat Davis, and for Don Doyle, who was there for that first Millersburg book 22 years ago and who is just as good a friend today.

Acknowledgments

Books like this are never written by a single author and I must gratefully acknowledge the help of the following who shared their glass with me: Preston VerMeer, Jack Beckwith, Bonnie and Rick Boldt, Mike Carwile, John and Lucile Britt, Bob and Pat Davis, Bob Gillespie, Rosemary Frey, Eugene Serbus, Donna Peavy, Phillip Hessenius, Rick and Debbie Graham, Richard and Merri Houghton, Carl Buehler Jr., Len and Kay Knotts, Mary Breeck, Eugene Reno, Michael Sturm, Helen Phillips, Ivan and Barbara Gignac, and anyone else I may have unintentionally overlooked. It's your book, too.

Author's Note

When I wrote the first edition of this book two years ago, I wasn't sure how it would be received by collectors of opalescent glass despite the enthusiasm for its predecessor, *The Standard Opalescent Glass Price Guide*. My worries proved to be groundless and I couldn't be happier with the response. In this volume I've added over 125 patterns as well as some new whimsies and a few additions to the late glass section. The prices have been updated and expanded and since my first efforts, opalescent glass regularly appears in major glass sales at premium prices, taking its rightful place in the field of glass collecting.

Again, let me thank my publishers who have put up with me since 1974, and give a special thanks to my editor, Lisa Stroup, and all the graphic designers and layout people who do such a great job. They are the best in the business.

Bill Edwards

Contents

Part I: Opalescent
Glass, 1880 – 1930
Page 8

Part II: Opalescent
Whimsies
Page 136

Part III: Opalescent
Glass After 1930
and Reproductions
Page 156

Introduction

From its inception in the 1880s opalescent glass has enjoyed a widely receptive audience, both in England where it was introduced and here in America where a young but growing market was ready for any touch of brightness and beauty for the hearth and home.

Early American makers, such as Hobbs, Brockunier and Company (1863 – 1888), Buckeye Glass (1878 – 1896), LaBelle Glass (1872 – 1888), American Glass (1889 – 1891), Nickel Plate Glass (1888 – 1893), and of course, the Northwood Glass Company in its various locations (1888 until its demise in 1924) were the primary producers, especially in early blown opalescent glass production. They were not by themselves, of course. Other companies such as Model Flint (1893 – 1899), Fostoria Shade & Lamp Co. (1890 – 1894), Consolidated Lamp & Glass (1894 – 1897), Elson Glass (1882 – 1893), West Virginia Glass (1893 – 1896), National Glass (1899 – 1903), Beaumont Glass (1895 – 1906), Dugan Glass (1904 – 1913) which then became Diamond Glass (1914 – 1931); and finally the Jefferson Glass Company (1900 – 1933) added their talents in all sorts of opalescent items in both blown and pressed glass.

The major production covered 40 years (1880 – 1920); however beginning shortly after the turn of the century the Fenton Glass Company of Williamstown, West Virginia, joined the ranks of opalescent manufacturers and has continued production off and on until the present time. Their production from 1907 to 1940 is an important part of the opalescent field and has been covered to some extent in this book. The Fenton factory, along with Dugan and Jefferson glass, produced quality opalescent glass items long after the rest of the companies had ceased operations, primarily in pressed items in patterns they had used for other types of glassware.

In 1899 A. H. Heisey & Company began *very* limited production of some opalescent glass in white and blue, by adding a milky formula to the glass while it was still in the mould. Patterns known are #1225 Pineapple and Fan in white and vaseline; #2 Plaid Chrysanthemum in vaseline (1904); #1220 Punty Band in white and blue (1904 – 1910); #1280 Winged Scroll in white (1910); #357 Prison Stripe in white (1905); #300 Peerless in blue; and a Pluto candlestick in experimental gold opalescent. Most of these were made in very small amounts for very short periods of time and by 1915 they were no longer in production.

To understand just what opalescent glass is has always been easy; to explain the process of making this glass is quite another matter. If the novice will think of two layers of glass, one colored and one clear, that have been fused so that the clear areas become milky when fired a second or third time, the picture of the process becomes easier to see. It is, of course, much more complicated than that but for the sake of clarity, imagine the clear layer being pressed so that the second firing gives this opal milkyness to the outer edges, be they design or the edges themselves, and the process becomes clearer. It is, of course, the skill of the glassmaker to control this opalescence so that it does what he wants. It is a fascinating process and anyone who has had the privilege of watching a glassmaker at work can testify to it being a near-miracle.

Today, thousands of collectors seek opalescent glass and each has his or her own favorites. Current markets place blown opalescent glass as more desirable, with cranberry leading the color field, but there are many ways to collect, and groupings of one shape or one pattern or even one manufacturer are not uncommon. When you purchase this glass the same rules apply as any other glass collectible: (1) look for any damage and do not pay normal prices for damage; (2) choose good color as well as good milky opalescence; (3) **Buy what pleases you!** You have to live with it, so buy what you like. To care for your glass, wash it carefully in lukewarm water and a mild soap; **Never put old glass in a dishwasher!** Display your glass in an area that is well lighted and enjoy it!

Who Made It?

Confusion abounds over the Northwood/National/Dugan connection, as well as the Jefferson/Northwood connection. In 1896 Harry Northwood, Samuel Dugan Sr., and his sons Thomas, Alfred, and Samuel Dugan Jr. came to Indiana, Pennsylvania, operating the Northwood Glass Company there until 1899, when Harry Northwood joined the newly-formed National Glass company combine. In 1903, he moved his operation to Wheeling at the old Hobbs, Brockunier plant and Thomas Dugan remained at the Indiana plant operating it as the Dugan Glass company.

From 1896 on, several patterns were produced as first Northwood, then National, and finally as Dugan; patterns such as Argonaut Shell/Nautilus, for example. There were many others that have previously been classified as either Northwood or Dugan that are actually Northwood/National/Dugan or even National/Dugan.

In addition we have certain patterns duplicated by both Jefferson and Northwood with little explination as to why moulds that were once Jefferson's then became Northwood's. Both companies were competitors, but examples of some patterns can be traced to both companies. It is also evident most patterns with a cranberry edging are really Jefferson, not Northwood as once believed.

Every answer raises new questions and in my 25 years of researching and writing about glass, I've learned that patience is the key. Answers come in their own time and at their own pace. One day we'll know most of what we question today and that is what drives us. I learn every day, mostly by contact with other collectors and so, I'm sure, do all of you.

Part I:
Opalescent Glass, 1880 – 1930

Abalone

Acorn Burrs

*A*balone

Found only in bowls with small solid handles, the Abalone pattern is believed to be from the Jefferson Glass Company and dates from the 1902 – 1905 period. Colors are blue, white, green, and rarely canary opalescent glass. The design, a series of graduated arcs in column, separated by a line of bubble-like dots, is nice, but nothing special.

*A*corn Burrs

Here is another of those well-known Northwood patterns that was made in the 1907 – 09 era in very limited opalescent glass production. Acorn Burrs is found in carnival glass in many shapes such as table sets, water sets, and berry sets. In opalescent glass it is limited to the small berry bowl shape and possibly the larger bowl (though none have been confirmed to date). Opalescent colors seem be just as limited and these small bowls are known in white and blue.

Alaska

Alva

*A*laska
One of the early Northwood patterns, Alaska dates from 1897, and can be found in a wide range of shapes including table sets, water sets, berry sets, a cruet, banana boat, celery tray, shakers, bride's basket. The tumblers and shakers are interchangeable with plain Fluted Scrolls and Jackson pieces. Colors are blue, white, vaseline, and emerald green as well as plain and decorated crystal.

*A*lva
This very impressive oil lamp is found in several variations including a blue opal stripe with frosted base and a vaseline stripe with the same base treatment. Dating to the 1890s, this lamp is quality all the way.

*A*rabian Nights
Dating from 1895 or 1896, this Northwood pattern, while confined to water sets and a syrup, can be found in white, blue, canary, and cranberry opalescent glass. The design (swirls, blossoms, and dots) combines the best of both Spanish Lace and Daisy and Fern and is a very striking pattern.

Arabian Nights

Arched Panel

Argonaut Shell

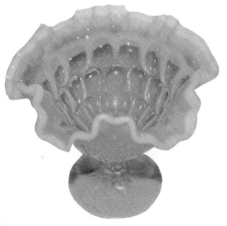

Argus (Thumbprint)

Arched Panel

This very attractive bowl in vaseline (light and airy) stands 4" tall and is 9" across. It is the master bowl to a berry set. The pattern has twelve wide panel sections around with a sharp outward turning at the base. There is a many rayed star on the base and the top edges are scalloped. I have no indication of the maker at this time, but I'd guess it is American and was made in other useful pieces like a table set. In many ways it reminds one of Imperial's Flute pattern

Argonaut Shell (Nautilus)

Originally a Northwood pattern, the opalescent examples were made by National or by Dugan after Northwood left National. Colors are blue, white, and vaseline and the shapes include water sets, table sets, berry sets, compotes, shakers, novelty bowls, and a cruet.

Argus (Thumbprint)

Many companies made similar patterns to this in pressed glass and while the closest American pattern is one called Argus, the compote shown may well be of English origin. Argus was made by Bakewell, Pears and Company around 1870 in crystal, and was made in a host of shapes. In the last few years, the Fenton factory has produced a similar compote from their Thumbprint line but the stem of the compote seems to be different. Any information on this piece would be appreciated.

Astro

Ascot

Typically British, this very striking pattern can be found in blue and canary opalescent glass by Greener in a complete table set as well as a biscuit jar. The design is strong with a filled bull's eye ringed and bordered by arcs.

Astro

Primarily a bowl pattern, Astro was made by the Jefferson Glass Company about 1905. It is a simple design of six circular comet-like rings on a threaded background above three rings of beads that are grouped from the lower center of the bowl upward. Colors are blue, green, white, and canary.

Aurora Borealis

Made by the Jefferson Glass Company and dating from 1903, this vase pattern is very typical of stemmed vases in the opalescent glass era. Rising from a notched base the stem widens with a series of bubble and scored lines that end in a flame-shaped top. From the sides are three handle-like projections, giving the whole conception a very nautical feeling. Colors are white, green, and blue opalescent.

Ascot

Aurora Borealis

Autumn Leaves

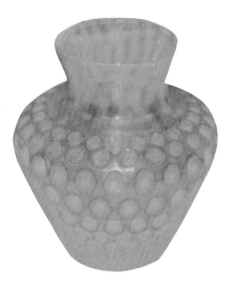

Baby Coinspot

Ball-Foot Hobnail

*Opalescent
Glass,
1880 – 1930*

Autumn Leaves

I am very drawn to this beautiful bowl pattern, attributed to the Northwood Company from 1905. The colors reported are green, white, and blue opalescent and the design is quite good with large, well-veined leaves around the bowl, connected by twisting branches and a single leaf in the bowl's center.

Baby Coinspot

While the well-known syrup in Baby Coinspot is from the Belmont Glass Company and dates from 1887, a newer copy is known by Fenton. The 7" vase shown does not appear to be a new item. The glass is thin and light and the color very soft. It may be that this vase is not American at all but a product of English origin, but I'm sure someone will write me about it. At any rate, it is a very attractive vase and certainly caught my eye.

Ball-foot Hobnail

So very little is really known about this pattern. It may have been a product of New Brighton Glass Company of New Brighton, Pennsylvania, but this hasn't been confirmed. The date of production seems to be around 1889 and most items are crystal while only a few have opalescence. The distinguishing points of identification seem to be the scallops on the edges and while some pieces do indeed have ball feet, others are collar based!

Banded Neck & Scale Optic

*B*anded Neck & Scale Optic

This very attractive small vase (5½" tall) is mould blown and has a pontil mark on the base. The scale optic pattern is on the inside and only the banding around the neck elevates this vase above the ordinary. I suspect it came in the usual colors but have only seen the white.

*B*arbells

Known only in the bowl shape, this rather undistinguished pattern has been credited to the Jefferson Glass Company in the 1905 – 06 period. The main design is a series of vertical ribs topped by a bullseye, with a smaller series of bullseyes below the ribs. Colors are blue, green, white, and canary.

*B*eaded Base Vase

Very similar to a design by the Northwood Company and shown in an old Butler Brothers ad, this attractive JIP vase is enameled with sprigs of flowers and has dots painted on the stem and around the base. If anyone has more information about this piece, I'd appreciate hearing from them. I'm sure it came in the usual opalescent colors.

Barbells

Beaded Base Vase

Beaded Block

Beaded Cable

Beaded Drapes

*B*eaded Block

Made by the Imperial Glass Company, the opalescent items date to 1913, but were made into the early 1930s. In carnival glass this pattern is called Frosted Block and is found mostly in marigold and clear iridized with a frosty look. Some pieces are signed "made in the USA." Opalescent items are found occasionally as evidenced by the creamer and sugar in vaseline.

*B*eaded Cable

This well-known Northwood pattern can be found in several treatments including opalescent, carnival, and custard. In opalescent glass, the colors are blue, green, white, and canary. Both rose bowls and open bowls are from the same mould. The design is simple yet effective and dates from 1904.

*B*eaded Drapes

This very attractive pattern is thought to be from the Northwood Company although examples with cranberry edging like some Jefferson items can be found. Dating from 1905, the pattern can be found on footed bowls, rose bowls, and banana bowls in blue, green, white, and vaseline.

Beaded Fans

Beaded Fans

Found mostly on footed rose bowls from the same mould as the bowl shown, this pattern is exactly like Shell and Dots minus the dotted base. Colors are white, green, and blue and the pattern dates from 1905. It has been credited to Northwood, but it is shown in Jefferson Glass ads as #211, so we know it is a Jefferson pattern.

Beaded Fleur de Lis

Attributed to Jefferson Glass, this stemmed compote can be found with the top opened out or turned in like a rose bowl. It was made in the 1906 era in blue, green, and white. The design is quite good and the base is very distinctive with three wide feet and beaded rings on the stems.

Beaded Moon and Stars

Just why the Fenton people made two patterns so very similar is a mystery but the other, Beaded Stars and Swag is shown elsewhere. Beaded Moon and Stars is often just called Beaded Stars. It came in bowls, a short-stemmed compote, and a banana bowl from the same mould. Colors are blue and white opalescent as well as carnival treatments.

Beaded Fleur de Lis

Beaded Moon and Stars

Beaded Oval in Sand

Beaded Star Medallion

Beaded Stars and Swag

Beaded Ovals in Sand

Originally called Erie this Dugan/Diamond pattern is very closely related to two other similar designs from this company. It can be found in water sets, table sets, berry sets, shakers, a cruet, a toothpick holder, and a ruffled small bowl. Found in blue, and white opalescent colors, the pattern was also made in apple green glass, blue, and crystal (sometimes decorated). Opalescent pieces are rather scarce.

Beaded Star Medallion

Often credited to the Imperial Glass Company in carnival glass, a recent find of marked marigold carnival pieces confirms this to be a Northwood pattern. In opalescent glass, it can be found in white, blue, and green. The pattern dates from the 1909 era and was made in both gas and electric shades.

Beaded Stars and Swag

The opalescent version of this pattern was made by the Fenton Glass Company in 1907. Shapes reported are bowls, rose bowls, and a rare plate. Both the bowl and the plate are known in advertising items (the plate is shown elsewhere) and are very rare. Colors found are white, blue, and green in opalescent glass, crystal, and carnival colors.

Beads and Bark

Beads and Bark

Shown as early as 1903, this Northwood pattern was made in their "Mosaic" or purple slag treatment, as well as appearing in opalescent colors of white, blue, and canary, as well as limited amounts of green. Like so many vases of the time the theme was a rustic look with tree limbs forming the supports to the base. In the case of Beads and Bark, these supports generate into a bowl that is a series of inverted loops with beaded edging forming three rows of design.

Beads and Curly Cues

Shown in a 1906 Butler Brothers ad with several other Northwood patterns including Leaf and Beads, Feathers, Wild Rose, Beaded Cable, Hilltop Vines, and others, this rather scarce footed piece can be shaped in several ways about the open-edged top. The piece shown is opened like a spittoon but the top has been seen standing up, pulled in, or slightly flared. Colors advertised are blue, green, or white.

Beads and Curly Cues

Beatty Honeycomb

Made by Beatty & Sons in Tiffin, Ohio, the Honeycomb pattern dates to 1888, and is also known as Beatty Waffle. Shapes found are a table set, water set, berry set, cruet, toothpick holder, celery vase, salt shakers, a mustard pot, individual cream and sugar, and the mug shape shown. Colors are white and blue opalescent. Be aware the pattern has been reproduced in the 1960s by the Fenton Glass Company in blue and an emerald green in vases, baskets, rose bowls, and a covered sugar.

Beatty Honeycomb

Beatty Rib

Beatty Swirl

Berry Patch

Beatty Rib

The A.J. Beatty & Sons Company originally made glass in Steubenville, Ohio, until they merged with U.S. Glass and moved their operation to Tiffin, Ohio, in 1891. Beatty Rib dates from 1889, and was made in both blue and white in a vast array of shapes including table sets, water sets, berry sets in two shapes, a celery vase, mug, nappies in assorted shapes, salt and pepper shakers, a mustard jar, salt dips, sugar shaker, toothpick holder, finger bowl, match holder, cracker jar.

Beatty Swirl

Like its sister pattern, Beatty Rib, this popular design was produced in 1889, in blue, white, and occasionally canary opalescent glass. Shapes known are table sets, water sets, berry sets, syrup, mug, water tray, and celery vase. Other pieces might well have been made including shakers, toothpick holder, cruet, mustard pot, and sugar shaker, so be aware of this possibility.

Berry Patch

Here is another of Jefferson's opalescent novelties that is delicate and quite simple in concept but very attractive. Mostly seen in small shallow bowls with a dome base, the design has occasionally been flattened into a dome-based plate that is most desirable. Colors are white, blue, and green opalescent and the pattern was originally Jefferson's #261, dating from 1905. The design is a simple series of stems, leaves, and berry clusters that ramble around the bowl.

Blackberry

While the pattern is sometimes called Northwood's Blackberry, I have no doubt it was a pattern produced by the Fenton Glass Company. It has been seen mostly in small sauce shapes but occasionally one of these is pulled into a whimsey shape. Colors in opalescent glass are blue, white, green, and a very pretty amethyst (another indication it is Fenton). It can be found in custard and opaque glass, and many times with a goofus treatment

Blackberry Spray

Very similar to the Blackberry pattern shown elsewhere, this Fenton design has less detail and more sprays. It is found primarily on the hat shape shown and usually in amethyst in opalescent glass or white. This same pattern and shape was made in carnival glass during the same time span and 1911 ads are known.

Blocked Thumbprint and Beads

While the history of this pattern tends to be confusing, mainly because it is only one step in a series of patterns done by the Dugan/Diamond Glass Company over a period of time, the study of two closely designed patterns sets the picture in order. Blocked Thumbprint and Beads and another pattern, Leaf Rosette and Beads, are very much alike. When you add a Dugan carnival glass item called Fishscale and Beads to the picture, you can see just why all three patterns came from the same maker. The latter is simply the original Blocked Thumbprint and Beads with an interior pattern of scaling! Opalescent colors are the typical white, blue, and green, but vaseline is a possibility.

Blackberry

Blackberry Spray

Blocked Tumbprint and Beads

Blooms and Blossoms

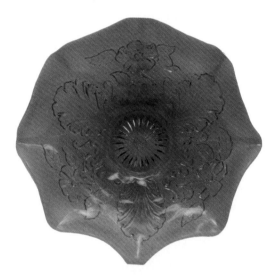

Blossoms and Palms

Blossoms and Web

Blooms and Blossoms

Also known as Mikado, this North-wood Glass pattern is known in several treatments including frosted glass with enameling, ruby stained with gilt, the flowers painted in an airy transparent coloring, as well as a goofus treatment. In opalescent glass the usual shape is this square-shaped nappy with one handle. It has been called an olive nappy and can be found in white, green, and blue opalescent colors. And if two names aren't enough, it can also be found as Flower and Bud in some books!

Blossoms and Palms

Credited to the Northwood Company, Blossoms and Palms dates to about 1905 and has been reported with the famous Northwood trademark. Colors are blue, white, vaseline, and green, and only bowl shapes have been reported. The design consists of three acanthus-like leaves with a stem of flowers and leaves between them.

Blossoms and Web

Very hard to find in any color, the white is most often found but a very scarce blue is shown here and an equally scarce green is known. The pattern is shown in a 1905 Northwood advertisement. The design of flowers connected by a webbing of stems is uncommon and more resembles Dugan patterns than Northwood; it continues down a stippled dome base to give a nice finish to the whole piece.

Blown Drapery

Made by Northwood as part of the National Glass combine in 1903, this very beautiful tankard water set and a companion sugar shaker are mould blown and can be found in white, blue, green, canary, and cranberry opalescent colors. Please compare this set with the later Fenton Drapery set shown elsewhere, for a complete understanding of just how this pattern varies from blown to pressed ware. Also, be aware that Blown Drapery has been reproduced in a cruet shape by L.G. Wright.

Blown Diamonds

What an outstanding piece of canary opalescent glass this 11½" tankard pitcher is. The pattern, much like Hobbs Opalescent Diamonds pattern is all interior. The applied handle is threaded and then twisted. I'm sure this pattern was made in other colors and I have a strong suspicion this pattern may be English, dating to the 1880s. If so, blue is a strong possibility. If anyone can shed more light on this piece, I'd appreciate knowing.

Blown Twist

Made by Northwood, operating as National Glass, this very scarce pattern is known in water sets and a sugar shaker. It dates from 1903 and the colors known are white, blue, canary, green, and cranberry. The handle on the water pitcher has a very unusual twisted look not found on other items in opalescent glass. Please note that the pitcher's mould is the same as that of Blown Drapery (both are blown items). A rare celery vase is known.

Blown Drapery

Blown Diamonds

Blown Twist

Boggy Bayou

Brideshead

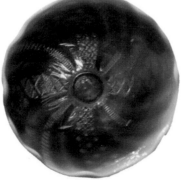

Broken Pillar (and Reed)

Boggy Bayou

Often confused with another Fenton pattern called Reverse Drapery, Boggy Bayou is found only on vase shapes. It can be found in opalescent colors of white, green, blue, and amethyst, in sizes from 6" to 13" tall. Production dates from 1907 in both opalescent glass and carnival glass. A Reverse Drapery vase whimsey is shown in the whimsey section and a comparison of the bases will help distinguish one pattern from the other.

Brideshead

This very well done English pattern was made by George Davison Company and bears the Rd #130643 identifying the pattern. Brideshead was made in water sets, table sets, a celery vase, and several bowl novelties in blue with the possibility of both white and canary existing. The pattern is one of alternating concave and convex columns that while simple is quite effective. As you can see, the opalescence is outstanding as is most from English makers.

Broken Pillar (and Reed)

Broken Pillar and Reed is credited to the Model Flint Glass Company of Albany, Indiana. The pattern dates from the 1902 – 1904 era and originally was called #909. In crystal, amethyst-flashed crystal, and a pretty amber-stained crystal, Broken Pillar and Reed was made in a complete table service as well as a jelly compote, however in opalescent glass, it has been reported only in the compote shape or, as shown, a stemmed card tray fashioned from the compote. Colors reported are white, vaseline, and blue in opalescent glass.

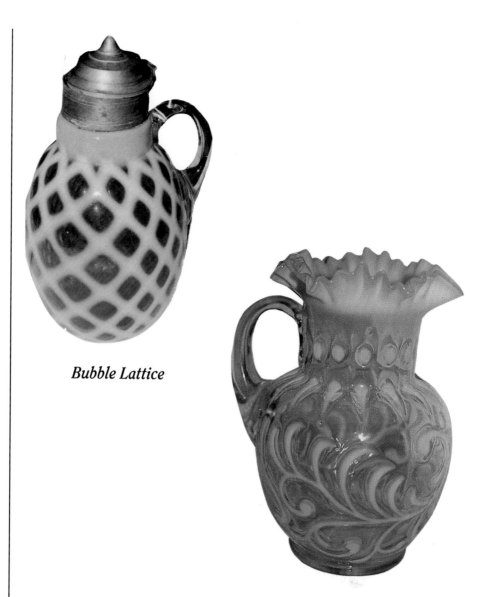

Bubble Lattice

Bubble Lattice

This pattern was called Plaid by Marion Hartung but is more commonly known as Bubble Lattice or simply Lattice. It was made in Wheeling by the Hobbs, Brockunier Company in 1889, and can be found in many shapes including water sets, berry sets, table sets, cruets, sugar shakers, syrups, toothpick holders, finger bowls, salt shakers, bowls, and bride's baskets. Colors are blue, white, canary, and cranberry and the finish was occasionally satinized.

Buttons and Braids

Credited to the Jefferson Company, Buttons and Braids dates to 1905 and has been reported in water sets and bowls in blue, green, white, and cranberry opalescent. Tumblers can be either blown or pressed. In addition to the colors listed there is a strange greenish vaseline that is very much like some of the Everglades pieces credited to Northwood, so this pattern may well have passed from the Jefferson Company to Northwood like others are known to have done.

Buttons and Braids

Button Panels

Here's a pattern first attributed to the Coudersport Tile & Ornamental Glass Company but shown in Northwood/National ads in 1902 – 03 and later shown in Dugan/Diamond ads in 1907 – 09. It has often been confused with a similar design called Alaska, but is found only in dome-based bowls and rose bowls. Colors are white, blue, canary, and very rarely green, with emerald known also.

Button Panels

Calyx

Cabbage Leaf

Casbah

Casbah

Cabbage Leaf

Exactly like the Winter Cabbage bowl shown elsewhere, except Cabbage Leaf has three large leaf patterns over the twig-like feet. This piece is usually turned up to form a very neat vase. Both patterns are from the Northwood Company and date from its 1906 – 07 period of production. Colors in the Cabbage Leaf pattern are white, green, and blue opalescent with canary a possibility.

Calyx

Once credited to the Northwood Company, this vase seems to be a product of the Model Flint Glass Company during their association with National. Colors are white, blue, and green opalescent but none is easy to find and I've been looking for a blue one for years. While Calyx is the most used name, a secondary title is Expanded Stem which no one seems to use nowadays. While the design is rather simple, the appeal is strong.

Casbah

Very much like Arabian Nights, Rococo, and Arabesque, this very pretty stemmed piece flattened from a compote seems to be English in origin. The stem has a knob that appears to be cross-hatched and the design inside the bowl of the compote is a series of opposing geometrics, four each making up eight panels. Shown in white, there is probably a blue and maybe a canary example out there. The design dates this piece to the 1890s.

Cashews

Cashews

More commonly found in goofus treatment than opalescent glass, this bowl pattern has been attributed to the Northwood Company. However, I have a hunch it was really made by Dugan after 1904, at the Indiana, PA, factory. Colors are white, blue, and green and the white can be found with some goofus treatment.

Cherry

Made by Bakewell, Pears and Company about 1870, the Cherry pattern was made in crystal as well as opalescent glass in many shapes including a scarce plate, goblet, berry set, table set, stemmed wine, open and covered compotes, and novelty bowls of several shapes. The cherry design is very realistic and the leaves form arcs.

Cherry Panel (Dugan Cherry)

Better known in carnival glass, this Dugan/Diamond pattern is often seen in peach opalescent glass. Other carnival glass colors are amethyst and marigold. In opalescent glass reported colors are white, blue, and canary. The example shown has a goofus treatment with the cherries done in red and the leaves in gold. Production dates to 1907 and the only shape reported in opalescent glass is the three-footed bowl, often shaped in a variety of ways.

Cherry

Cherry Panel

Chippendale

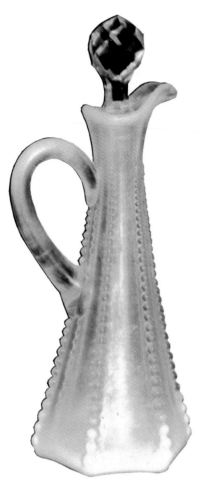

Christmas Pearls

Christmas Snowflake

*C*hippendale

This very pretty pattern was a product of George Davison and Company, England, and dates to 1887. Shapes known are baskets, compotes, and tumblers, so I suspect a jug or pitcher of some shape was made. Colors are blue and canary and both are top notch as the photo clearly shows.

*C*hristmas Pearls

Occasionally called Beaded Panel (it isn't the same as the Beaded Panels pattern often called Opal Open), this quite rare and beautiful pattern is most likely a Jefferson Glass design that dates from 1901 – 1903. The only shapes reported are the cruet shown and a salt shaker. The colors known so far are blue, white, and green opalescent.

*C*hristmas Snowflake

Originally a Hobbs, Brockunier pattern, Christmas Snowflake was a lamp pattern produced by that company in 1891. In 1888, Northwood began production in water sets (both plain and ribbed), as well as, a cruet and possibly a vase. In 1980 a reproduction was made by L.G. Wright of the plain water set, as well as new shapes (sugar shaker, barber bottle, basket, rose bowls in two sizes, syrup, milk pitcher, cruet, brides bowl, and a creamer). The original lamps were made in three sizes in blue, white, and cranberry. The Northwood water set was made in the same colors and the cruet in white only.

Chrysanthemum (Base) Swirl

First made at the Buckeye Glass Company of Martins Ferry, Ohio, this design became one produced by the Northwood Company in a speckled finish. Buckeye production dates to 1890 in white, blue, and cranberry, sometimes with a satin finish. Shapes are water sets, table sets, berry sets, a cruet, syrup, sugar shaker, toothpick holder, salt shaker, finger bowl, celery vase, mustard, and a beautiful straw holder with lid. The speckled treatment was patented by Northwood and except for this look, the shapes are the same.

Chrysanthemum Swirl Variant

Here is a very scarce variant pattern, credited to the Northwood Company by some. It has even been called a mystery variant. In size and make-up, the tankard pitcher is much like Ribbed Opal Lattice, also credited to Northwood from 1888; however if you examine the color of the pitcher here you will find it anything but typical of that company. It isn't blue or even green, but a very strong teal. It can also be found in white and cranberry. It is possible the design was first made elsewhere and Northwood produced later versions.

Circled Scroll

A Dugan Glass product, Circled Scroll dates from 1904 and can be found in carnival glass, opalescent glass, and a soft green glass. Shapes known are the water set, berry set, table set, cruet set, jelly compote, and salt shaker but not all colors are found in each treatment. In the carnival items, a whimsey vase, pulled from a tumbler is also known but none have been reported in opalescent or apple green treatments.

*Chrysanthemum
(Base) Swirl*

*Chrysanthemum
Swirl Variant*

Circled Scroll

27

Cleopatra's Fan (Northwood's Shell)

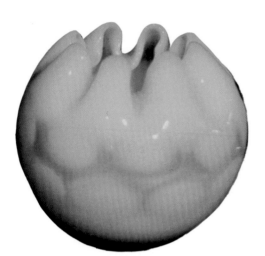

Coinspot (Jefferson)

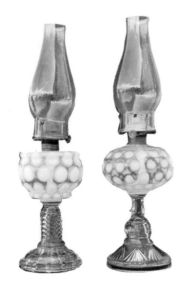

Coin Dot Lamps

Coin Dot Lamp

C leopatra's Fan (Northwood's Shell)

After a series of names, the latest seems to be "Cleopatra's Fan" so we'll settle on that one. Known in white, blue, and green opalescent glass, this pattern is actually a product of Dugan/Diamond and was never a part of the Northwood line. It is quite scarce and collectible.

C oin Dot Lamps

Shown are three very distinctive oil lamps in the Coin Dot pattern. The largest lamp is called Inverted Thumbprint and Fan base and dates to 1890. It can be also found in blue opal. The other table lamp is called Chevron Base and is shown in a 1893 U.S. Glass ad, made by King Glass of Pittsburgh. I strongly suspect the small hand lamp was from the same company since they have the same font shape. Other colors were made in both of these I'm sure.

C oinspot (Jefferson)

I believe this previously unreported rose bowl was made by Jefferson from their salad bowl (Jefferson's #83). This company also made the water set (#180) in white, blue, green, and cranberry which was later copied by the Fenton Company. Please note the base which has been ground first.

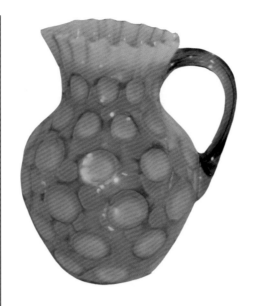

Coinspot (Northwood)

Coinspot (Northwood)

Shown is the Northwood water pitcher with the star-crimp top. These water sets were made at the Indiana, PA, plant and production was probably continued when Dugan took over the plant. Butler Brothers catalog ads show this pitcher in 1903 – 1904 from the Northwood/National production. Colors are white, blue, green, and cranberry.

Coinspot Syrup

While it is, at best, difficult to distinguish some moulds of one company from those of another, I truly believe the syrup shown is from the West Virginia Glass Company and the same shape can be found in their Polka Dot items where the dots are colored rather than opalescent. At any rate, I'm sure these pieces were made in white, blue, cranberry, and possibly other colors since some Coinspot items are also found in green, amber, vaseline, amberina, rubina, and even amethyst.

Coinspot Water Bottle

In addition to all the other Coinspot items we've shown, I just couldn't resist showing this very scarce water bottle shape. The glass is very light weight and delicate and it has been seen in cranberry opalescent glass, as well as, this white example. While I haven't been able to confirm the maker of this item, I'm confident it is old and quite scarce.

Coinspot Syrup

Coinspot Water Bottle

29

Colonial Stairsteps

Compass

Concave Columns (#617)

Colonial Stairsteps

Although mostly found on this toothpick holder shape, a breakfast set consisting of a creamer and sugar are also known. Colors are crystal and blue opalescent only and although the breakfast set has been reported with the Northwood trademark, none have been seen to date so the attribution is a bit shaky at this time.

Compass

While this pattern has been identified as Reflecting Diamonds in one publication, it definitely is not. Compass, while similar, has eight large overlapping arcs that make up the key elements of the design while Reflecting Diamonds is a series of graduated petal shapes that contain inverted rays, files, or diamonds topped by more fan rays. Only the marie or base design of the two patterns is the same. Compass is found (very rarely) on bowls and plates in green or blue opalescent and as the exterior of carnival glass bowls with Heavy Grape as the primary design. The plate shown is marked with the Diamond-D mark.

Concave Columns (#617)

As stated elsewhere (see Pressed Coinspot), this pattern was originally called #617 in a 1901 National Glass catalog and was later continued by Dugan/Diamond Glass in an ad assortment in the compote shape. For some strange reason, the vase has become known as Concave Columns. The compote, in opalescent glass is known as Pressed Coinspot and in carnival glass is simply called Coinspot. Shapes from the same mould are vases, compotes, goblets, and a stemmed banana boat shape. Colors in opalescent glass are white, blue, green, and canary.

Constellation

Shown in a 1914 Butler Brothers ad for Dugan/Diamond Glass Company this very scarce compote was reported to be available in both white and blue opalescent. Originally the mould for this piece was the S-Repeat goblet (the pattern was originally called National and was a product of Northwood/National Glass that dated to 1903). When Dugan obtained the National moulds, the exterior pattern became S-Repeat and the goblet was turned into a compote with a pattern on the interior called Constellation. In addition to the few opalescent items, many shapes were made in colored crystal with gilding, as well as a few shapes in carnival glass including the compote where the S-Repeat exterior is known as Seafoam! Another example of name complication that plagues collectors.

Coral

Found only on bowls with odd open work around the edging, the Coral pattern may well be a product of the Jefferson Company. Colors are the usual: white, blue, green, and vaseline. And while it has the same name as a Fenton carnival glass pattern, the design is far different.

Coral Reef

While most collectors have lumped this pattern with Seaweed it truly is a different pattern and it took a letter from a collector and an article by John D. Sewell to set me straight on this pattern. Seaweed has branches and distinct round dots while Coral Reef (Mr. Sewell's name) has a rambling line pattern with square-type extensions rather than dots. Coral Reef can be found in bitters bottles, barber bottles (round or square), finger bowls, lamps in four sizes including a mini night lamp, a stemmed oil lamp, a finger lamp, and a stemmed finger lamp.

Constellation

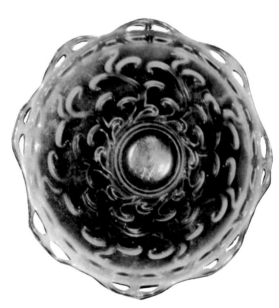

Coral

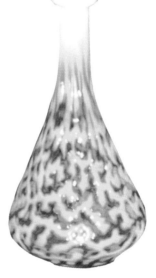

Coral Reef

Cornith

Cornucopia

*C*ornith

Standing 11" tall, this very nice vase has the twelve ribs so often associated with the carnival vases called Cornith. Since Westmoreland made many of the iridized ones, I suspect this vase is from the same factory. It may well have been made in other colors and I'd guess the time of production to be in the 1910 – 1915 era.

*C*orn Vase

Despite having been reproduced by Wright Glass in the 1960s, this beautiful Dugan pattern is a collector's dream. Dugan made it in 1905 in white, blue, vaseline, and a rare green, as well as, a super-rare marigold carnival. The mould work is fantastic and the open husks show real glassmaking skill.

*C*ornucopia

This very attractive Northwood novelty vase dates to 1905, and can be found in white or blue opalescent glass. While it has been reported in carnival glass, I've never seen an example in my 26 years of collecting. The design is a nice one, almost like a basket weave that flares to handles on two sides while the rolled bottom rests on a decorative base.

Corn Vase

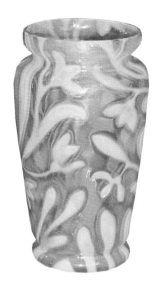

Crocus

Crocus

Recently, this vase was sold at an auction and was listed as Daffodil vase. When the owners examined it, they found it was different in pattern entirely from the Daffodil pieces and appears to be a pattern previously unlisted. The design resembles a crocus so we've named it that. As you can see, the coloring is not a true blue but a strong turquoise tint. The vase stands 6½" tall and has a 2¾" base diameter. I feel this pattern is either Northwood or Dugan/Diamond but can't be positive at this time.

Curtain Optic

Fenton began making this very pretty design in 1922 and continued for several years, adding a medium wide striped opalescent pattern called Rib Optic. These patterns were made in several pitcher sizes and shapes along with iced tea tumblers, handled tall tumblers, and handled mugs. Even a two-piece guest set (small bedside pitcher and tumbler) can be found. Usually, the handles on both pitchers and mugs were of a darker glass. Some of these opalescent items were iridized.

Curtain Optic

Daffodil

Shown in a couple of 1906 ads in a Lyon Brothers catalog along with other Northwood pattern water sets, it seems this pattern was continued by the Dugan Company after Northwood left the Indiana, PA, factory. The pitchers are in two shapes, bulbous or a slimmer tankard, and colors known are white, canary, green, and blue. There is also a variant pitcher which has fewer blossoms and foliage that appears to be Northwood's also.

Daffodil

Dahlia Twist

Dahlia Twist Epergne

Daisy and Drape

Dahlia Twist

Made by the Jefferson Glass Company around 1905, Dahlia Twist was originally Jefferson's #207 pattern. It is a typical cone-shaped vase on a circular base with a flared and ruffled top. The real interest comes in the ribbing that is twisted against an interior optic that runs in the opposite direction. Colors are the typical white, green, and blue opalescent.

Dahlia Twist Epergne

I am thrilled to show this very beautiful epergne as it was originally sold. Most collectors believe this Jefferson Glass lily had a glass dome-based bowl as a holder, but the lily was made expressly for decorative metal holders as shown in ads of the day. Most were silvered but a few were gilded as the one shown. The lily came in the usual opalescent colors and a similar lily and metal holder in the Fishnet pattern was sold by the Dugan/Diamond Company.

Daisy and Drape

Well known to carnival glass collectors, this Northwood pattern stands 6½" tall. In design it much resembles a U.S. Glass pattern called Vermont and may well have been a Northwood copy. Nevertheless, this is the first known Daisy and Drape vase in opalescent glass and I can't begin to tell you just how rare and important a find it is. We can only hope someone had the good sense to produce other colors. A blue would be a super find.

Daisy and Fern (Apple Blossom Mould)

Daisy and Fern (Apple Blossom Mould)

Never reproduced like many other Daisy and Fern items, Northwood's Apple Blossom Mould line can be found in several shapes including a spooner (shown), creamer, sugar, and night lamp. Colors are blue, white, and cranberry. The spooner shape also doubled as a pickle caster insert.

Daisy and Fern

Here is the small rosebowl shape in this pattern without Northwood's Swirl or the Apple Blossom shaping. Daisy and Fern was made at several locations over a period of time so placing certain pieces becomes a task. Let us just say West Virginia Glass, Northwood (alone and part of National), and Dugan all made this pattern, and in recent years, the Fenton factory made pieces for Wright. Colors known are white, blue, green, and cranberry opalescent in old items and canary in repos.

Daisy and Greek Key

Very little seems to be known about this pattern. In opalescent treatment it can be seen on these small footed sauces in white, blue, or green. The daisy design runs around the top and covers the base and the Greek key bands the piece. Production is in the 1900 – 1910 period, I'm certain. Some collecters feel this pattern is from Canada but I can't confirm this.

Daisy and Fern

Daisy and Greek Key

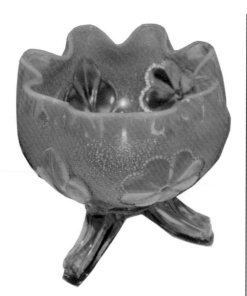

Daisy and Plume

Daisy Dear

Daisy in Criss-Cross

Daisy and Plume

While this famous design was made for years under the Northwood/National banner, the example shown comes from the Dugan Company, despite having no holes in the legs. The mould work is excellent and there is no Northwood marking. Colors are green, white, and blue opalescent glass and carnival glass. Dugan ads date from 1907 on this footed rose bowl.

Daisy Dear

Daisy Dear is better known as a carnival glass pattern made by Dugan/Diamond. This exterior design for medium size bowls isn't too imaginative but manages to fill a good deal of space. The pattern in opalescent glass is on a collar base bowl in white, green, or blue. Production dates to 1907 – 1909. The pattern of four sparse blossoms and leaves that go outward from a daisy-like base design has fern-type leaves as well as spade-shaped ones.

Daisy in Criss-Cross

Made by Beaumont Glass in 1895, this rather scarce pattern can be found only in watersets and a syrup in white, blue, and cranberry opalescent. The pitcher shown has the so-called "ring-neck" design as does the syrup. The tumblers are flat based and straight-sided. Daisy in Criss-Cross has not been reproduced so it is very collectible.

Daisy May

Daisy May

Made by the Dugan/Diamond Company, this very attractive nappy is a kissin' cousin to the Leaf Rays pattern found in carnival glass. On Leaf Rays the pattern is interior while on Daisy May the design is all exterior and shows through the glass nicely. It has been shown in 1909 ads and the few examples that I've seen are blue opalescent despite being advertised in white also.

Daisy Wreath

I am extremely pleased to show this very rare item from the Westmoreland company. It is usually found in carnival glass on a milk glass base, but here we have a rich blue glass with opalescent edges. The bowl is 9" in diameter and is the only example in opalescent glass I've seen without iridescence.

Daisy Wreath

Desert Garden

This novelty dome-base bowl pattern can be found in white, blue, or green opalescent glass. The design of three sets of leaves bracketing a stylized blossom with a stippled background isn't very imaginative, but does fill most of the available space. The example shown, like most, has a ribbon-candy edging that adds to the appearance. The maker hasn't been determined but I lean toward Dugan/Diamond.

Desert Garden

Diamond and Daisy

*Diamond and Oval
Thumbprint*

Diamond and Daisy (Caroline)

Ads in a 1909 Butler Brothers catalog identify this pattern as part of the Intaglio line from the Dugan Company. It is clearly shown in a handled basket shape, so we know at least two shapes were made. Dugan first advertised the Intaglio line in 1905, and it included painted plain crystal as well as blue, green, and white opalescent. The pattern of Diamond and Daisy is very similar to the Wheel and Block pattern. Known as "Caroline" in carnival glass.

Diamond and Oval Thumbprint

This very attractive design, found only on the vase shape, is from the Jefferson Glass Company, circa 1904. It can be found in white, blue, or green opalescent glass and may vary in size from 6" tall to 14".

Diamond Maple Leaf

Attributed to the Dugan Glass Company (Dugan/Diamond), this hard to find two-handled bon-bon can be found in green, white, and blue opalescent. The design shows rather realistic maple leaves flanked by very flowing scroll designs that give the piece a real artistic look. Diamond Maple Leaf dates from 1909.

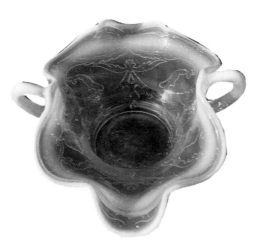

Diamond Maple Leaf

Diamond Optic

*D*iamond Optic

I know very little about this attractive piece except it is from England. I base this on the finish and shaping. It may be known by another name also, but I felt this name summed up the configuration as well as any. The diamond pattern is all on the inside and runs from the outer rim to a middle diameter above the stem. It can be found in white opalescent also, and may well have been made in canary or vaseline.

*D*iamond Point

Found only on the vase shape, this Northwood pattern dates from 1907, and can be found in white, blue, and green opalescent glass and many carnival glass colors. Sizes range from 8" to a lofty 14" that has been swung to reach that size.

*D*iamond Point and Fleur de Lis

Since this pattern is shown in a 1906 Butler Brothers ad showing other Northwood patterns including Beaded Cable, a Diamond Point vase, Leaf and Beads, Spokes and Wheels, and Wild Rose, there is little doubt of the maker. In addition, it can occasionally be found with the Northwood trademark. Colors are white, blue, and green opalescent and the shapes are bowl novelties.

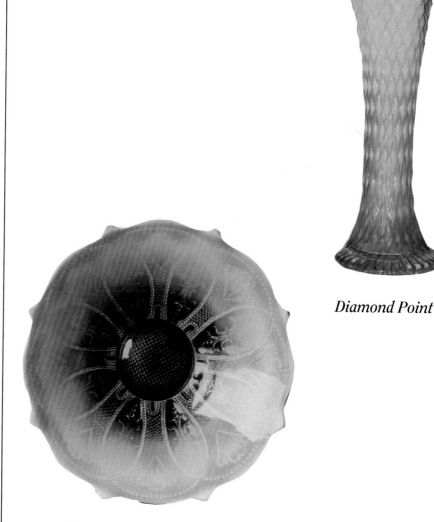

Diamond Point

Diamond Point and Fleur de Lis

Diamond Stem

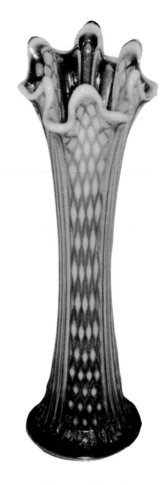

*Diamond Point
Columns*

Diamond Spearhead

Diamond Point Columns

While many carnival glass collectors are familiar with this pattern and associate it with the Imperial Glass Company of Bellaire, Ohio, it was also a product of the Fenton Company and is shown in Butler Brothers ads with other Fenton patterns. In opalescent glass, only the vase has been reported and I am very happy to show an example of this rarity. This opalescent piece stands 12" tall and was made in 1907.

Diamond Spearhead

First produced by Northwood as part of the National Glass line (#22) as early as 1901, this very nice geometric pattern can be found in table sets, water sets, goblets, berry sets, a toothpick holder, mug, syrup, salt shaker, decanter, celery vase, tall (tankard) creamer, jelly compote, a tall (fruit) compote, and cup and saucer, 10" plate, water carafe, relish tray, and spittoon whimsey. Creamers are found in several sizes and two sizes in the water pitcher are known. Colors known are green, white, vaseline, blue, sapphire blue, and plain crystal glass.

Diamond Stem

Although credited to both Model Flint Glass and Northwood, it is hard to imagine two companies sharing such a simple pattern. The interior and exterior swirls run in opposite directions. The diamond prism above the base is the identifying design. Colors are white, vaseline, a rare blue, a rare aqua, and a reported green. Shapes may vary, especially the tops, but I haven't seen this pattern shaped into a bowl or compote. As you can see there are two sizes in Diamond Stem. The usual size is 6½" tall with a 2⅝" base diameter while the larger size is 8¼" tall with a 2⅞" base.

Diamond Wave

*D*iamond Wave
First thought to be English or European glass, the origin of this unique pattern remains blurred. The covered pitcher has shown up in amethyst opalescent as well as the cranberry coloring previously known. Now we add a 4¾" vase to the mix. All pieces are mould blown with very rich opalized work.

*D*iamonds
Made by Hobbs, Brockunier & Company, this cute bud vase dates from 1888. In addition to being opalescent, it has an added coralene decoration of flowers and leaves in the tiny glass beading that was so popular at the time. Usually found on water pitchers (two shapes), in cranberry, this vase is a real rarity. It is only 5" tall.

Diamonds

*D*ogwood Drape
I once heard this pattern referred to as Dogwood Drape so I am using that name despite no real information about it. The design looks to be British and has that strong opalescence on the high-styled stem. The compote's bowl has a series of feathered drapes above stippled blossoms and leaves with a rayed pattern extending to the stem. If English, it may have been made in both blue and canary. Anyone knowing more about this piece is encouraged to contact me.

Dogwood Drape

Dolly Madison

Dolphin

Dolphin and Herons

Dolly Madison

From the Jefferson Glass Company, this 1907 pattern can be found in water sets, table sets, berry sets, plates, and novelty bowls, in blue, green, and white opalescent, as well as crystal and a strong electric blue glass. It was originally known as Jefferson's #271. The design, while not brillant, is attractive with its wide panels seperated by sections of flower and leaf sprigs.

Dolphin

Originally made by the Northwood Company as early as 1902, this beautiful compote has been widely reproduced in all colors, so buy only what you are confident with. Colors are white, blue, and vaseline. The older compotes have a stronger color and better glass clarity but those are about the only differences.

Dolphin and Herons

A product of the Model Flint Glass Company of Albany, Indiana, while a part of National, this hard-to-find novelty can be seen in both a compote shape or flattened into a stemmed tray. The stem is the dolphin, turning back on its tail, almost swallowing the bowl which has herons and fauna. Colors are white, blue, and canary in opalescent glass as well as crystal.

Dolphin Petticoat

Shards of these lovely candlesticks have been found at the Indiana, Pennsylvania, factory dump site and the pattern is shown in a National Glass ad, so we know the Northwood Company made these while a part of the National Combine. Colors are white, blue, and canary. The mould work is outstanding, as is the design.

Dolphin Petticoat

Double Greek Key

Made in Fostoria, Ohio, by the Nickel Plate Glass Company and then continued by U.S. Glass, this very attractive pattern dates to 1892. Shapes known are table sets, berry sets, water sets, a celery vase, toothpick holder, mustard pot, pickle dish, and salt shakers. Colors are white and blue opalescent, as well as plain crystal.

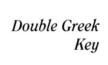

Double Greek Key

Double Stem Rose

While this famous Dugan/Diamond pattern is very well-known in carnival glass, the example shown is the first in opalescent glass I've seen. It has to be quite rare. The pattern dates from 1910, and I'm sure this bowl was an early product. As you can see, it has the very typical Dugan one-two-one crimp and may well show up in other opalescent colors including blue and green, and each of these would be equally rare.

Double Stem Rose

Drapery (Fenton)

Drapery (Northwood)

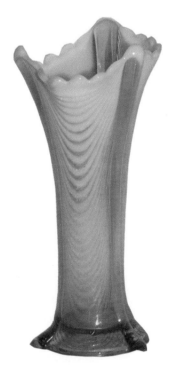

Drapery Vase

Opalescent
Glass,
1880 – 1930

Drapery (Fenton)

While the Blown Drapery pattern was made at the Northwood Company, the Fenton example is mould-blown and dates to 1910, five years later than Northwood's. In addition, the Fenton version has a shorter, ball-shaped pitcher while the Northwood version is tankard shape. Fenton Drapery colors are the usual white, blue, and green opalescent with amethyst being a possibility.

Drapery (Northwood)

Sometimes called Northwood's Drapery, this interesting pattern dates from 1904, and usually is marked. Colors are white and blue opalescent, often with gold decorated edges and ribbing. Shapes known are table sets, water sets, berry sets, and some novelty items including a rose bowl. Some of the shapes were carried over into carnival glass production; these include rose bowls, candy dishes (from the same mould), and the vase shape.

Drapery Vase

If you will examine the Drapery pattern made by the Northwood Company you will see this vase is theirs also and was made in several types of glass including opalescent, carnival, and crystal. Some people call this vase a whimsey but they were literally made by the hundreds, so they are not true whimsey pieces. Colors are blue, white, green, and canary.

Double Dolphin

Double Dolphin

This is Fenton's #1533 pattern and the opalescent production was very limited. Dating to the 1920s, colors I've verified are blue or white (Fenton calls this French opalescent). This dolphin design was, of course, one of the company's favorites and has been used in many shapes and sizes for 75 years.

Dugan's Daisy Intaglio (Western Daisy)

In 1905 the Dugan Glass Company began producing a line of glass in crystal and opalescent white that had a goofus treatment. The following year they added colors to this line. It was advertised in 1909 as their intaglio line and it included the pattern shown, which is known in carnival glass as Western Daisy and in opalescent glass as Daisy Intaglio. Colors are blue, green, and white, often with a goofus treatment.

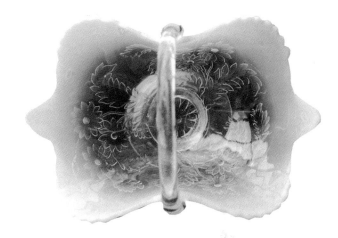

**Dugan's Daisy Intaglio
(Western Daisy)**

Dugan's Diamond Compass (Dragon Lady)

As I said in the first edition of this book, this pattern has been confused with two other Dugan patterns, namely Reflecting Diamonds and Compass. There are differences and if you will compare the photos you will see changes in both the collar base (marie) and the pattern designs. Green and white opalescent are the reported colors, but blue was surely made.

**Dugan's Diamond Compass
(Dragon Lady)**

Dugan's Hexagon Base

Dugan's Hexagon Base

This very pretty Dugan vase with the hex base and the jack-in-the-pulpit turned top, stands 7½" tall. The coloring is very good and the mould work excellent. This vase was made in white and green opalescent, and perhaps with a ruffled top. It dates from the 1907 – 1910 period.

Dugan's Intaglio

Designed in 1904 for a line of mostly goofus ware, Dugan's Intaglio designs were primarily fruit patterns (very rare examples of flowers and birds exist) that had a gold and colored treatment to the leaves and fruits while the rest of the glass remained crystal. Fruits found are cherries, grapes, strawberries, and plums, while flower patterns were mostly roses and poppies. Not all of these pieces had opalescence but a few did; we are showing a very pretty Cherries bowl which had red fruit and gilt leaves.

Dugan's Intaglio Grape

As part of the Dugan Intaglio line, this beautiful 13" chop plate can be found with or without opalescent treatment and has been seen with gilding and enamel work. Many of the patterns in this line, some shown elsewhere in this book, have been found in colors of green or blue opalescent and it is possible this grape pattern may have been made in colors too. The pattern is all exterior and is intaglio.

Dugan's Intaglio

Dugan's Intaglio Grape

Dugan's Junior (Jack-in-the-Pulpit Vase)

If you will compare this Dugan vase to the stemmed Dugan Jack-in-the-Pulpit shown elsewhere you will see both have a wide ribbed exterior and are shaped exactly the same. This one is flat. Base-hand measures 4½" tall while the hex-based one measures 7½" tall. The Junior is known in the usual opalescent colors of white, blue, and green.

Dugan's #1013 (Wide Rib)

Shown in 1905 Butler Brothers ads along with other Dugan/Diamond products, this nice vase hasn't much in the way of design but is long on opalescence. It is often very widely flared at the top with opal running from the flames down between the ribs. Colors reported are blue, green, white, and canary, but I've never seen the canary. This vase was also made in carnival glass, often twisted. Shown are two sizes of the vase as well as a bowl whimsey from the same mould.

Dugan's Olive Nappy

In a Butler Brothers 1906 ad, this piece is called a fancy handled olive and was listed available in white, blue, and green opalescent glass from the Dugan/Diamond Company. It measures some 4¾" across from handle to opposite edge and is on a flat base. Since there is no interior or exterior design it relies on shape and glass finish for whatever appeal it has.

Dugan's Junior
(Jack-in-the-Pulpit Vase)

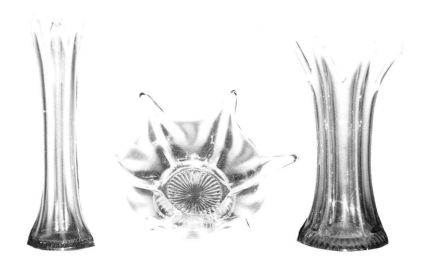

Dugan's #1013 (Wide Rib)

Dugan's Olive Nappy

Dugan's Peach Intaglio

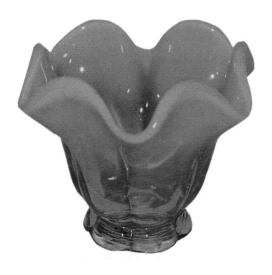

Ellen

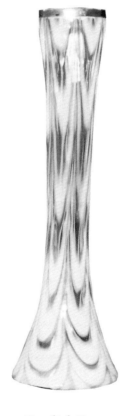

English Drape

Dugan's Peach Intaglio

Like the other patterns in the Intaglio line, this design of peaches is a companion piece to the grape plate that is also 13" in diameter. Notice this piece still has the goofus treatment as well as opalescence and is just a super exterior design. Intaglio pieces came in all shapes including plates, baskets, bowls, and compotes and in many sizes.

Ellen

I've been able to learn little about this beautiful 5" vase. It is of very thick, clear glass and has six wide panels on the exterior that extend from below the rim to the scalloped base. The opalescence is quite heavy and rich. I've seen this vase in white and green but expect a blue exists. Unable to find a name, I've called it Ellen in honor of my mother.

English Drape

This very attractive vase with a gilded top stands 9¾" tall and has a base diameter of nearly 2". It is thin glass and looks much like opalescent products from England so I've taken liberty with the name. If anyone has additional information on this pattern, I'd appreciate hearing about it. I would suspect white and blue examples were also made.

Estate

Shown in a 1906 Butler Brothers catalog with other Dugan patterns, this unusual 4½" vase was advertised in white, blue, and green opalescent glass. These do not have the normal stippling associated with the carnival glass version and perhaps we should really call it Dugan Estate to separate it from the Westmoreland Estate pattern that is similar. At any rate, the Dugan Estate piece should be considered a real find in opalescent glass for they are quite scarce in any color.

Estate

Everglades

Originally called Carnelian, this Northwood pattern dates from 1903. It was made in several treatments beside opalescent glass including custard and purple slag. Opalescent colors are white, blue, and canary, with some limited production in green. Shapes made are table sets, water sets, berry sets that are oval in shape, cruets, salt shakers, and jelly compotes.

Everglades

Everglades (Cambridge)

Everglades is a production name used by the Cambridge Company covering a line of items made from 1920 to the 1930s. The compote shown in white opalescent glass is simply one design from this line. It measures 7½" in diameter. In 1933, the Cambridge catalog listed 43 items in this line called Everglades, including vases with flower patterns, and a bowl with an Indian on horseback hunting buffalo. The line was made in many treatments and colors from 1924 to 1958.

Everglades (Cambridge)

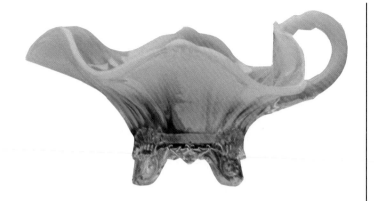

Fan

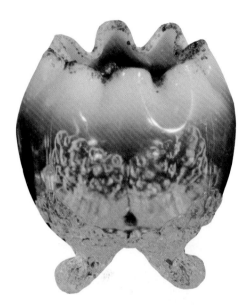

Fancy Fantails

Feathers

*F*an

Long considered a Northwood pattern, Fan is actually from the Dugan/ Diamond plant, shown in a 1907 company ad in water sets, berry sets, and table sets in ivory (custard) and opalescent glass in colors of green, white, and blue. In a whimsey plate that was shaped from the spooner, the glass almost glows with opalescence. Fan was also made in emerald green and cobalt blue, sometimes with gold decoration, as well as, limited shapes in carnival glass.

*F*ancy Fantails

While others credit this pattern to the Northwood Company, I'm convinced it is from Jefferson. As I've said before, research has convinced me most (if not all) of the cranberry decorated items came from Jefferson Glass. Fancy Fantails dates from 1905, and can be found in both rose bowls and candy dishes from the same mould. Colors are white, blue, green, and vaseline.

*F*eathers

No question about the maker of this vase since most are marked with the Northwood trademark. Vases are the only shape, and the colors are white, blue, and green opalescent, as well as, carnival glass colors. Sizes range from 7" to a pulled 13". I've seen a blue opalescent and a white opalescent vase with gold edging.

Fenton's #220 Stripe

*F*enton's #100 (Ringed Bowl)

Made first in 1929, this small bowl on stubby feet measures 7½" across and the plate from the same mould is ½" wider. Colors in opalescent glass are amethyst and vaseline, but I suspect others were made. The only pattern is the exterior rings that extend from the feet up the sides of the piece.

*F*enton's #220 Stripe

Found in iced tea sets (both pitcher and tumblers have contrasting colored handles) and nights sets (tumble-ups), this was a popular Fenton pattern, produced in 1929. Colors are blue, green, white, and vaseline, and there are two shapes and sizes in pitchers. Note that the one shown has a matching lid but not all shapes do.

*F*enton's #370

This beauty dates from the 1924 – 1927 period of Fenton production. The cameo opalescent coloring is a real treat and I'm happy to be able to show this example. This same coloring can be found in many patterns and shapes in the Fenton line including bowls, vases, nappies, and bon-bons. The base color of the glass is a strong amber and the opalescence is a rich creamy tint.

*Fenton's #100
(Ringed Bowl)*

Fenton's #370

Fenton's Vintage (Leaf)

Fern

Fine Rib (Fenton)

Fenton's Vintage (Leaf)

Seen mostly in carnival glass, this very distinct Fenton pattern dates from 1909 – 10 and can be recognized by its large leaf center as well as the five bunches of grapes that are grouped around the bowl. The exterior is plain, as is the marie. Colors reported are white, blue, and a rare amethyst. All colors are hard to find and well worth the search.

Fern

From several makers including West Virginia Glass, Beaumont Glass, Model Flint Glass, and possibly Northwood, this pattern is much like Daisy and Fern without the daisy. Shapes are water sets, cruets, salt shakers, syrups, sugar shakers, toothpick holders, a covered butterdish, a covered sugar, a creamer, a spooner, berry sets, a celery vase, a finger bowl, a mustard pot, and a bitters bottle. Colors are white, blue, and cranberry opalescent. It dates from 1898 to 1906 depending on the maker. Fenton has also reproduced this pattern in the 1950s.

Fine Rib (Fenton)

I'm very happy to be the first to show this very rare Fenton vase pattern in opalescent glass. Until now, the Fine Rib vase was well known in carnival glass and scarce in plain colored pieces such as ice green and pink. But as you can see, the pattern was made in a beautiful vaseline opalescent treatment. This vase stands 11¹/₃" tall with a 2⁷/₈" base and a 3⁵/₈" top opening. The opalescence runs well down the ribs and is just stunning! I believe this vase was made in the 1908 – 1910 era and there may well be white, blue and green examples that exist. I'm very much in the debt of Craig and Brenda Kuckelburg for sharing this rare find.

*F*inecut and Roses

Early opalescent production of this pattern was at Jefferson's Steubenville plant, however Northwood later produced this pattern in their lines of custard and carnival glass. Colors in opalescent glass are white, blue, and green. Shapes (all from the same mould) are footed candy dishes, rose bowls, and a shape called a spooner that is slightly ruffled.

*F*ish-in-the-Sea

There is a good bit of doubt about the origin of this very strong pattern but both Northwood and Dugan/Diamond are strong possibilities. It has been found with some goofus decoration which both companies used, but it has a European look. Colors are white, blue, and green. This vase is a scarce item, much sought by collectors.

*F*ishscale and Beads

Usually found in carnival glass, this Dugan/Diamond pattern is a rather scarce item in opalescent glass. The "fish-scales" are on the interior and the string of beading on the outside. Colors are mostly white or blue but I certainly wouldn't rule out vaseline or green. If you look closely, you will see a close resemblence to the Blocked Thumbprint & Beads pattern, also made by Dugan/Diamond. The same mould exterior was used for both.

Finecut and Roses

Fish-in-the-Sea

Fishscale and Beads

Flora

Fluted Bars and Beads

Floral Eyelet

*F*lora

Dating from 1898 this Beaumont pattern can be found in a host of shapes including table sets, water sets, berry sets, shakers, cruets, syrups, toothpick holders, compotes, celery vases, and several bowl novelty shapes. Colors are blue, white, and vaseline with some items gilded. Other types of glass were also made in Flora including crystal and emerald green, which can also be found with gilding.

*F*loral Eyelet

Little is known about this very scarce pattern; it is believed to be a product of Northwood/National or even Dugan at the Indiana, Pennsylvania, plant. The time of production has been speculated from 1896 to 1905 with the only shapes being a water pitcher and tumbler in white, blue, and cranberry opalescent. The tumbler is shown here. The reproduced pitcher, made by the L.G. Wright Company, is shown elsewhere in this book. The new pitchers have reeded handles while the old do not.

*F*luted Bars and Beads

While previous writers have credited this very interesting pattern to the Northwood Company, I am convinced it is a Jefferson Glass Company product, dating to 1905 or 1906. The colors in opalescent glass are white, blue, green, and vaseline, often with a cranberry edging (a reason to suggest Jefferson as the maker). The design is a simple one of two sections of threading and beads that border a center area of fluting.

Fluted Scrolls (Jackson)

Originally called Klondyke, this multi-titled pattern is known today as either Fluted Scrolls or Jackson. It was first advertised in 1898 by the Northwood Company and can be found in table sets, water sets, berry sets, cruets, salt shakers, a puff box (also called "baby butter"), two-piece epergne, and various bowl shapes. Colors are blue, white, and vaseline opalescent as well as custard, green, and crystal glass. Sometimes this pattern is decorated, giving rise to still another name, Fluted Scrolls with Flower Band. Currently being reproduced.

Fluted Scrolls with Vine

Shown as early as 1899 in a Butler Brothers ad, this Northwood Glass Company pattern is one of my favorite vase designs. It is known in white, blue, and canary and may also show up in green one of these days. I am constantly amazed at the colors and patterns that have been overlooked for years. The design of flowers, stems, and leaves winding around a fluted, cone-shaped vase is very pretty when you add the base of spread leaves and the top rim of scalloped blossoms, the whole piece becomes a real work of art.

Forked Stripe

If you look at the base of this barber bottle, you'll see the stripes end in points so I've given it a name. This piece is white opalescent, measures 7" tall and has a base diameter of 3½". It is marked on the base "PAT-PENDING." The maker isn't known at this time but a pitcher from a very limited Imperial Glass production in 1930 has this same pointed finish to its stripe except it is reversed and faces upward. Other colors probably exist, but I can't be sure.

Fluted Scrolls

Fluted Scrolls with Vine

Forked Stripe

Four Pillars

Four Footed Hobnail

Frosted Leaf and Basketweave

*F*our Pillars

Made by the Northwood Company (Dugan/Diamond later made this same vase in carnival glass), the Four Pillars vase can be found in white, blue, green, and possibly vaseline in opalescent glass. The identifying features are the four columns of glass that run from top to bottom ending in toes and the ribbing between these columns. Vases can be found from 9" to 13" tall and a few have been seen with gilding.

*F*our-Footed Hobnail

Found only in table set pieces, all with the strange peg feet, this pattern remains somewhat of a mystery. In opalescent glass, the colors are blue (dark), white, and canary but it was also made in crystal, vaseline, and blue glass. More than likely the date of production was in the early 1900s but the maker remains unknown, at least to me.

*F*rosted Leaf and Basketweave

Credited to Northwood, this pattern seems to be found only in the table set pieces. It dates to 1905 and the colors known are blue, vaseline, and white opalescent, as well as crystal. Interestingly enough, the exterior pattern of the famous Rose Show bowls match this pattern exactly without the leaf and I suspect the spooner mould was retooled to make this fine bowl exterior.

Gonterman (Adonis) Hob

Gonterman (Adonis) Hob

Like the Swirl pattern with the same titles, this is a Aetna Glass pattern dating to 1886 (despite bearing "Pat'd Aug 4, 1876" on the base). Unlike the Swirl pattern, there doesn't seem to be a blue version, only the amber. Needless to say, since only the cruet shown has been reported, it is extremely hard to find and has to be considered rare.

Gonterman Swirl

Attributed to Aetna Glass Company, this very attractive pattern dates to 1886, and can be found in table sets, water sets, berry sets, cruet, syrup, celery vase, lamp shade, and a toothpick holder (sometimes in a metal frame). Pieces can be found with a blue or amber top edge while the base can be opalescent or frosted. While some items are signed "Patented August 4, 1876," this is not the date of production and probably refers to a design patent by Louis Wagner covering the fusing process used to create this pattern.

Gossamer Threads

Mould blown, this hand decorated finger bowl has been seen in a ruffled bowl and a matching 6½" plate all in blue with the cranberry threading. The glass is light and very thin and the example shown measures 4" wide and 2½" tall. I have a strong feeling this glass may be European but it is, without question, quality all the way.

Gonterman Swirl

Gossamer Threads

Grape and Cable

Grape and Cherry

Grape and Vine

Grape and Cable

Very little production of this pattern in opalescent glass is found besides the rare bon-bon in the last edition and several shapings of this large footed fruit bowl (some are turned like a centerpiece bowl). The bon-bon has been reported in vaseline only while the footed bowl has been seen in white, vaseline, and suspected in blue. The bon-bon may have been made in white also and carries the famous Northwood basketweave as the exterior pattern. In addition, the Fenton Company made a Grape and Cable large fruit bowl nearly identical to Northwood's. It is found in white opalescent also.

Grape and Cherry

While most writers list this nice bowl pattern as being from an unknown maker, I'm convinced it is a pattern that was made by the Sowerby Glass Works of England. I base this on years of experience with carnival glass from both American and foreign makers; Grape and Cherry in carnival glass have frequently been associated with British production. In opalescent glass, it is found in white, canary, and blue only, another hint of English origin. At any rate, it is a nice pattern with alternating ovals of grapes and cherries with a neat scrolling and torch design separating the sections.

Grape and Vine

I haven't been able to learn a thing about this very pretty pattern, but the owner calls it Grape and Vine so I'll stick with that name until I learn differently. It reminds one of Panelled Grape but on close examination it isn't the same at all. The Jack-in-the-Pulpit shape makes it special, and I'm sure it came in other colors.

Grapevine Cluster

Every time I see one of these imaginative vase patterns from the opalescent age, I am amazed by the artistic abilities in their design. Grapevine Cluster is another Northwood pattern, dating from 1905. It has a grape leaf base, twig supporting branches, and realistic grapes in a cluster. Colors are the usual white, blue, and vaseline or canary but it can also be found in non-opalescent purple slag from the Mosaic line.

Grapevine Cluster

Grecian Urn

The owner of this small pretty vase (4¼" tall with a 2" base diameter) named this piece and it seems to fit. I believe this piece may be English but I could be wrong. The opalescence is outstanding. I'd be interested in hearing from anyone who knows more about this pattern or can tell me of other colors.

Grecian Urn

Greek Key and Ribs

This Northwood bowl pattern is similar to the Greek Key and Scales bowl shown below. Dating from the 1907 production, the dome based bowl can be found in white, blue, green, and canary, as well as the host of carnival colors. Just why one company would create two moulds so similar is a mystery but it seemed to happen frequently, especially in opalescent and carnival glass. Perhaps competition forced so many variations but I can't be sure. At any rate, it makes collecting more interesting for all of us.

Greek Key and Ribs

Greek Key and Scales

Harrow

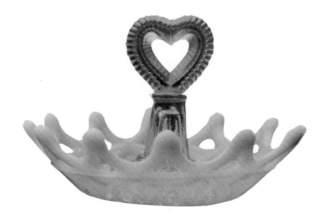

Heart Handled Open O's

Greek Key and Scales

Made by the Northwood Company in 1905, this often marked pattern is well-known in both opalescent glass and carnival. The bowl shape has a dome base and is usually ruffled. Opalescent colors are white, green, and blue.

Harrow

This English pattern has been unnamed to the best of my knowledge so I've taken the liberty of calling it Harrow. It stands 6" tall and bears an RD #217749. It was probably made in table set pieces, and a stemmed wine or cordial has been seen. Colors besides blue probably include white and canary.

Heart Handled Open O's

While this is primarily the same pattern as the Open O's we show elsewhere, the handled ring basket has always been shown on its own and we will keep it that way. It is a Northwood pattern, dating from 1905 – 06. Colors are white, blue, and green, with canary a strong possibility.

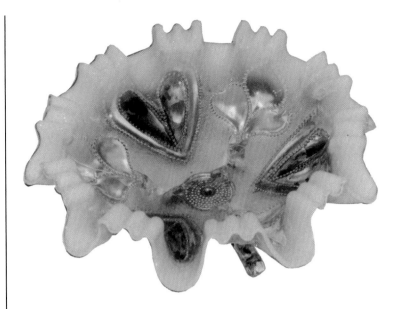

Hearts and Clubs

Hearts and Clubs

This Jefferson Glass Company pattern was originally their #274 and was produced about 1905. As you can see the footed bowl shown here has a goofus treatment, but it can be found on blue and green opalescent glass as well. The three feet of the bowl are shaped like those on the Daisy and Plume pieces made by Northwood and later Dugan, but are solid without any portholes.

Hearts and Flowers

This well-known Northwood pattern can be found in carnival, custard, and opalescent glass. In the latter, it is seen on compotes and bowls in white, blue, and very rarely vaseline. Production dates from 1908, when the maker added several well-known patterns to their opalescent production on a limited basis, including Singing Birds, Peacock on the Fence, Rose Show, Grape and Cable, Three Fruits, Bushel Basket, Acorn Burrs, Beaded Cable, Finecut and Roses, and Daisy and Plume. All were made mainly in white or blue, with a few vaseline items.

Heatherbloom

From Jefferson Glass, circa 1905, and called their #268, this seldom discussed pattern is found only on vases. Colors in opalescent glass are the usual white, blue, and green with the latter hardest to find. The design has a tendency to blur as the vase is swung to taller sizes and only the shorter ones really show the pattern at its best.

Hearts and Flowers

Heatherbloom

Heron and Peacock

Herringbone (Plain)

Herringbone (Ribbed)

Heron and Peacock

While I have very little information about this child's mug, known as Heron and Peacock, I believe it to be an old example. I've been told it has been made in many glass treatments over the years and is listed in one book on children's collectibles as having once been made in crystal and cobalt blue, but this is the first I've actually seen. It may well have been made in other opalescent colors and a blue or canary one would be outstanding. The design has a peacock on one side and the heron on the other with floral sprays dividing them. The opalescence is quite good. It is currently being reproduced by Boyd Crystal Art Glass, Cambridge, Ohio.

Herringbone (Plain)

Since shards of this pattern were found at the Indiana, PA, plant, we can be confident one of the makers of Herringbone (both plain and ribbed) was the Northwood Glass Company. Shard colors were white, yellow, and blue, but of course, cranberry items are also known. Items known are water sets, cruets, syrups, and crimped salad bowls. Some treatments are cased mother-of-pearl in a satin finish. The plain Herringbone dates to 1885, when Harry Northwood was at the Phoenix Glass concern.

Herringbone (Ribbed)

As I said in the narrative about plain Herringbone, this is most likely a Northwood pattern, found on water sets, cruets, syrups, and crimped salad bowls in white, blue, cranberry, and canary opalescent glass. While the plain Herringbone came first and dates to Northwood's days at Phoenix, the ribbed Herringbone is believed to date to about 1902, at the Indiana, PA, plant. Since I felt the two treatments were so different, I believe they should be discussed as separate items.

Hilltop Vines

Hilltop Vines

This unusual compote is shown in Northwood ads as early as 1906, so we know who made it. It can be found in white, blue, and green opalescent glass and stands roughly 5" tall. Outstanding features are the leaves that overlap, making up the bowl of the compote, the branch-like legs that form the stem, and the domed base covered with tiny bubble-like circles.

Hobnail (Hobbs)

Here is the Hobnail from Hobbs, Brockunier. Shapes made in this well-known pattern are water sets, table sets, berry sets (square shaped), cruets, shaker, syrups, finger bowls, celery vase, barber bottle, water tray, bride's basket with frame, and five sizes of pitchers. Production of the Hobbs Hobnail design began in 1885 and lasted until 1892. Colors reported are white, blue, rubina, vaseline, and cranberry.

Hobnail (Hobbs)

Hobnail and Panelled Thumbprint

Most collectors consider this pattern to be Northwood and I certainly agree. It dates to 1905, can be found in white, blue, and canary, and can be found in berry sets, table sets, and water sets. The tumblers have no thumbprints and are therefore harder to recognize. Other pieces may exist but I am unaware of them.

Hobnail and Panelled Thumbprint

Hobnail-in-Square

Holly & Berry

Honeycomb (Opal)

Hobnail-in-Square

Made by the Aetna Glass and Mfg. Company of Bellaire, Ohio, this pattern dates from 1887 and is often confused with a recent pattern called Vesta made by the Fenton Company since the 1950s. Colors for the original pattern are primarily white but it was also made in crystal. Shapes are water sets, table sets, berry sets, a celery vase, salt shakers, and compotes.

Holly & Berry

Unreported in opalescent glass until now, this Dugan/Diamond pattern is quite well known in carnival glass in bowls and the attractive nappy shape. The design shows berries and three leaves in the bottom and a wreath of leaves and berries around the body of the bowl. These nappies are generous in size, measuring 7" across from handle to tip. The only color reported to date is white but surely blue and green have been made.

Honeycomb (Opal)

Sometimes called Opal Honeycomb, I've heard this vase referred to as Hobbs Honeycomb also, despite there being no proof as far as I know that it was made by Hobbs. Colors known are blue or white opalescent but green or vaseline are certainly strong possibilities. Besides the honeycombing, the chief design factor is the ribbed-skirt base.

Honeycomb and Clover

*H*oneycomb and Clover

Made by the Fenton Company in several types of glass including carnival, opalescent, and gilt decorated. Production in opalescent glass dates from 1910, and the colors known are the usual white, blue, and green. However, amethyst is a definite possibility and would be a real find. The pattern is exterior and consists of an all-over honeycombing with clover and leaves twining over it. Shapes in opalescent glass are water sets, berry sets, table sets, and novelty bowls.

*I*dyll

Made by Jefferson Glass, Idyll can be found in water sets, table sets, berry sets, a toothpick holder, cruet and salt shakers sometimes grouped on a tray, and an intermediate size bowl. Colors in opalescent glass are blue, green, and white, and the pattern can also be found in crystal, gilded green, and blue. Idyll dates from 1907.

Idyll

*I*nside Ribbing

Beaumont Glass of Martin's Ferry, Ohio, made this very pretty glass in early 1900s, and while it isn't plentiful, many times it is overlooked. Colors are white, canary, blue, and possibly green, the shapes are berry sets, table sets, water sets, toothpick holders, a cruet, a syrup, salt shakers, a cruet set, and a celery vase. Some pieces have enameled decoration adding to the interest.

Inside Ribbing

Intaglio

Intaglio

One of Northwood's earlier patterns, dating from 1897, in custard production, Intaglio was made in a host of shapes including table sets, water sets, berry sets, a cruet, salt shakers, a jelly compote, and many novelty shapes. Colors made in opalescent glass are white, blue, and occasionally canary, but other treatments such as gilded emerald green and, of course, custard are available.

Interior Panel

This very nice Fenton vase dates from the early 1920s and besides the fine example in amber opalescent, I've seen it in Cameo opalescent, iridized stretch glass in Celeste Blue, Velva Rose, and Florentine Green; all from the 1921 – 1927 era of production. The same mould was used to make a trumpet vase also. The example shown is 8" tall and has a fan spread of 5".

Interior Swirl

Much like the Inside Ribbing pattern but with a twist, this very pretty rose bowl is perfectly plain on the outside and has a ribbing that has been twisted on the interior. Notice the cranberry frett along the top indicating this pattern is most likely from Jefferson Glass. One writer dates this pattern to the 1890s but I'd place it closer to 1904 or 1905. The canary coloring is quite good and the base prominent.

Interior Panel

Interior Swirl

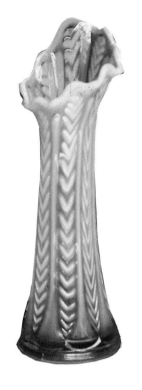

Inverted Chevron

Inverted Chevron

When I first saw this very attractive vase, I thought it was Plume Panels, a pattern well-known to carnival glass collectors. But on close examination, it is very different. I suspect it may be from Jefferson Glass and I've named it Inverted Chevron. While blue and green are the only colors I've seen, I'm sure it must have come in white.

Inverted Fan and Feather

First made by Northwood in other treatments including custard glass (Dugan/Diamond made the opalescent items), Inverted Fan and Feather can be found in water sets, table sets, berry sets, a jelly compote, punch sets, a toothpick holder, a salt shaker, a rare cruet, and many whimsies that include spittoons and rosebowls. Opalescent colors are white, blue, green (rare), and canary and Dugan also made a few items in carnival glass.

Iris with Meander

Iris with Meander is also known as Fleur-de-Lis Scrolled and is a product of Jefferson Glass, dating to 1902 or 1903. It was made in table sets, water sets, berry sets (two sizes of sauces), toothpick holder, salt shaker, jelly compote, vase, pickle dish, and the plate shown. Colors are flint, blue, canary, green, and rarely amber opalescent, as well as crystal, blue, green, and amethyst glass with decoration.

Iris with Meander

Inverted Fan and Feather

Jackson

Jazz

Jackson

May I say I personally hate not calling this pattern and Fluted Scrolls by the original name that covered both patterns, Klondyke, but I will bow to previous writers. Jackson is a Northwood pattern and can be found on table sets, water sets, berry sets, cruets, candy dishes, and a mini-epergne. Colors are white, blue, canary, and limited amounts of green. It was also made in custard glass.

Jazz

While I can't find this pattern pictured in any Dugan/Diamond ad, I feel sure it came from that company. Note the base has two levels and the unusual treatment of the top is sassy and bold, so I've named it Jazz and I feel that it is certainly a descriptive title. Shown in blue, it probably came in white and green also. Date of production should be in the 1906 – 1909 time frame, I'd bet. It is 6" tall.

Jefferson #270 (Jefferson Colonial)

At first glance this looks like another Jefferson pattern called Iris With Meander. Indeed, the moulds may have been the same, for this design is missing the fleur-de-lis at the base and the beading in the slots. Shown is the master berry bowl in blue so we know the berry set was made. Colors are surely the usual Jefferson ones of white, blue, green, and canary and I'd like to hear from anyone who has additional information about shapes and colors.

Jefferson's #270

Jefferson Shield

Jefferson Shield

This very rare pattern was from the Jefferson Glass Company, produced as their #262 pattern. It is a dome-based bowl, found in green, white, and blue opalescent. It has a series of 13 shields around the center of the bowl. If you are the owner of one of these bowls, consider yourself very lucky, for less than one dozen in all colors are known!

Jefferson Spool

This very unusual vase by the Jefferson Glass Company looks as if it were turned on a lathe. It stands approximately 8" tall and was made in 1905. Colors reported in opalescent glass are white, green, blue, and vaseline. No other shapes have been seen, but it could easily have been opened into a compote.

Jefferson Spool

Jefferson Stripe

This very pretty Jack-in-the-Pulpit vase in opalescent Stripe has a pretty cranberry edging that is a giveaway to its maker — the Jefferson Company. It has a collar base and stands 8½" tall. As you can see, the coloring is almost an emerald green and the opalescent striping goes all the way down the base. It was made in white and blue.

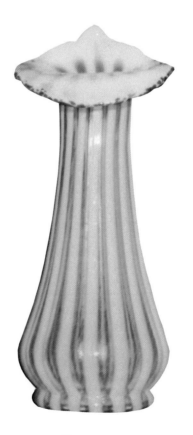

Jefferson Stripe

Jefferson Wheel

Jewel and Fan

Jewel and
Flower

Jefferson Wheel

This very attractive bowl dating from 1905 is, as the name implies, another pattern from Jefferson Glass. It was originally Jefferson's #260 pattern and can be found in white, blue, or green opalescent glass. It has been reported in carnival, but I seriously doubt that possibility.

Jewel and Fan

Jefferson made a lot of opalescent glass and here is still another pattern which was originally identified as their #125. It is found on bowls and an elongated banana bowl in white, blue, green, and rarely canary. The design is simple but very effective.

Jewel and Flower

Made by the Northwood Company in 1904, and originally called Encore, this very attractive pattern can be found on water sets, table sets, berry sets, cruets, and salt shakers. Colors are white, blue, and canary, often decorated with gilding as in the example shown. Incidentally, there is a variant with the design going all the way to the base and eliminating the beading and threading band.

Jewelled Heart

Long credited to Northwood, Jewelled Heart (or Victor, as it was originally called) was first made by Dugan in 1905. Shapes available are table sets, water sets, berry sets, a syrup, sugar shaker, a condiment set consisting of cruet, salt and pepper shakers, and toothpick holder on a round flat tray or plate. Colors in opalescent glass are white, green, and blue, but the pattern is also found in carnival glass, crystal, green, and blue decorated glass, and very rarely ivory or custard glass. Some items are marked with the Diamond-D marking.

Jewels and Drapery

This very pretty Northwood vase dates to 1907, and can be found in ads from that year. As you can see, the drapery is very well done with a tiny tassel ending between the folds. Around the base are a series of jewels or raised dots. Strangely, in a Northwood ad in a 1906 Lyons Brothers catalog, there is a similar vase shown that has an additional row of pendants below the jewels. The ad is labeled the Fairmont opal assortment. To date I haven't seen any examples of this vase.

Jolly Bear

Now known to be a Jefferson Glass Pattern, this pattern was made in the 1906 – 08 era. It is reported in white, blue, and green opalescent, sometimes with gilding; however, I've only seen it in the white. There is a carnival glass pattern in very scarce water set pieces called Frolicking Bears which looks a good deal like the Jolly Bear bowl. Frolicking Bear is from the U.S. Glass Company. Jolly Bear was shown in a 1908 Jefferson ad.

Jewelled Heart

Jewels and Drapery

Jolly Bear

Keyhole

King Richard

Lady Caroline

Keyhole

Also shown in 1905 Dugan Glass Company ads is the Keyhole pattern. It can be found in opalescent glass on bowls that have a dome base in white, blue, and green; and painted or goofus treatment on the white. A few years later, it was adapted for use as the exterior of carnival glass bowls with Raindrop pattern as an interior and on a very rare marigold bowl where the exterior is plain and Keyhole became the interior pattern.

King Richard

The owner of this very attractive compote named it and I have no argument with the name since I haven't been able to find it listed anywhere. It appears to be a British pattern, with an unusual stem of scrolled supports. The interior has an equally appealing pattern of swirling branches and leaves as well as a file shield with scroll edging. If anyone knows more about this pattern, I'd certainly like to hear from them. The compote is 4" tall, 6¾" wide, and has a 2⅝" base.

Lady Caroline

Another Davison pattern, this very cute English item was once believed to be made only in blue opalescent, but as you can see, a very pretty canary item is shown. Shapes known are baskets, a breakfast set consisting of creamer and sugar, and the neat little three-handled whimsey shown. No larger table set items have been reported and no pieces with the Rd number usually found on British glass. The pattern dates from 1891, when it was advertised as Patent Blue Pearline (apparently when blue was the only color!).

Late Coinspot

Here is a Fenton version of the famed Coinspot. This one dating from the 1925 – 29 era was called an iced tea set in advertising, and had a taller tumbler with it. Colors were white, blue, and green. As you can easily see, it has a semi-cannonball shape and the handle is rather thick. In 1931 Fenton made this same pitcher with a dark, contrasting handle, and teamed it with mugs with the same handle treatment.

Lattice and Daisy

Shown in a Butler Brothers ad in 1914 that features several Dugan Glass patterns in opalescent glass, the Lattice and Daisy tumbler was apparently the only shape in this pattern offered in this type of glass. In carnival glass, the complete water set, as well as a berry set, are shown. The opalescent colors listed in the ad for this tumbler were white and blue, but as you can see, a very rare vaseline was made. Strangely, the iridized glass production of this pattern was also 1914, so it may just be that the opalescent pieces were made to fill the packing amounts needed for shipment, since all items in the opalescent ad are considered quite scarce. They include the Mary Ann vase, the Windflower bowl, the Stork and Rushes mug, the Constellation compote, and Fishscale and Beads items.

Lattice Medallions

This very graceful pattern is from the Northwood Company and is sometimes marked with the famous "N." Found primarily in bowl shapes, often very ruffled and ornately shaped, Lattice Medallions can be found in the usual opalescent colors of white, blue, and green. Shown is a very pretty white opalescent bowl with the tri-corner shaping.

Late Coinspot

Lattice and Daisy

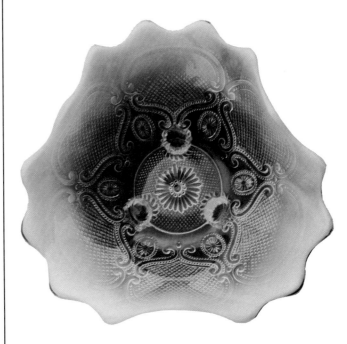

Lattice Medallions

Lattice and Points

Laura (Single Flower Framed)

Laurel Swag and Bows

Lattice and Points

This Dugan pattern is pulled from the same mould that producing the Vining Twigs plates and bowls that were made in carnival glass (as were the vases). In opalescent glass, the vases are usually short and haven't been pulled or swung as most vases are. Colors are white, mostly, but scarce blue examples are known and I suspect green was made also. Production of the opalescent pieces date from 1907.

Laura (Single Flower Framed)

Here is another example of poor naming; the Laura name is from Rose Presznick but the pattern has long been called Single Flower Framed by carnival glass collectors. It is a Dugan pattern, found only on the exterior of nappies, bowls, and this very rare ruffled plate. Colors previously reported are white and blue opalescent, as well as carnival colors (especially peach opalescent), but as you can see, this plate is in a very pretty green opalescent. These scarce items date from the 1909 period of Dugan production.

Laurel Swag and Bows

While I've searched every reference I could find about this pattern, it doesn't seem to be shown in any. We know it was made by the Fenton Company about 1908 for they made the only amethyst opalescent glass at about that time. As you can see there are laurel swags tied with a ribbon and bow, as well as cosmos-like flowers and an unusual bull's eye with a swirl of leaves connecting. I would appreciate any information about this pretty gas shade.

Leaf and Beads

Leaf and Beads

Just why Northwood made two variant treatments to this pattern is unclear but both are shown here. One has twig feet and a few changes in leaves while the other has a dome base. The latter should be called a variant. Production of the twig-footed bowl began in 1905, but by 1906 both styles were being advertised. Colors are blue, white, and green opalescent plus custard glass and carnival pieces.

Leaf and Diamonds

Here is another Dugan/Diamond pattern that can occasionally be found with a goofus finish. The bowl measures 9" across and has the typical Dugan 3-1-3 edge scalloping. There are three large spatula feet. It can be found in white, blue, and occasionally green. Strangely, the pattern is almost a companion to the Hearts and Clubs pattern made by Jefferson.

Leaf and Leaflets

Here is another of those patterns that appeared first in Northwood's lineup (1907 ads) and later became part of the Dugan production line. The opalescent examples in blue, white, and goofus are Northwood, however the same mould turns up later as a Dugan carnival glass pattern called Long Leaf in a beautiful peach opalescent iridized bowl. In addition, Long Leaf can be found as the exterior design for bowls and baskets of the Stippled Petals design in peach opalescent, also made by Dugan!

Leaf and Diamonds

Leaf and Leaflets

Leaf Chalice

Leaf Rosette and Beads

*L*eaf Chalice

Made by Northwood while a part of the National combine, Leaf Chalice appears in a May, 1903, Butler Brothers ad that featured three shapings of the piece. Colors usually found are white or blue, but green was also made as you can see and is considered a rare color in this pattern.

*L*eaf Rosette and Beads

Made by the Dugan/Diamond Company beginning in 1906, this pattern seems to be a cousin to Blocked Thumbprint and Beads with the addition of the chain of leaves added. And if you take a look at the Single Poinsettia pattern you will see just how similar these patterns are. Leaf Rosette and Beads is a scarce pattern and was most likely made in the usual colors but the only ones I've seen are white and green.

*L*ined Heart

Dating from 1906, this Jefferson Glass Company vase pattern can be found in white, blue, and green opalescent glass. The examples shown haven't been swung as many are and are about 7" tall; some range to 14" however.

Lined Heart

Linking Rings

*L*inking Rings

This British pattern was made by Davidson about 1895, and can be found in a water set, juice glass, bowl, and compote but I suspect a table set as well as a platter shape exist. The only color I've seen is a deep blue with very strong opalescence. Most pieces bear the Rd number 237038, typical of British glass.

*L*ion Store Souvenir (Beaded Stars Advertising)

Why so very few of these Fenton advertising pieces exist or why there are so very few advertising items in all of opalescent glass is a real mystery. The only pieces reported in Beaded Stars are one bowl and two plates. They read: SOUVENIR LION STORE HAMMOND. All three items are in blue.

*L*ittle Nell

Despite being very plain, this vase is still a very cute item. Except for the threading above the collar base, there is no design at all and whatever the vase has going for it comes from the shaping and fine opalescence. The maker isn't certain at this time and I'm not sure it really matters. Colors are white, blue, and green opalescent.

Lion Store Souvenir (Beaded Stars Advertising)

Little Nell

Little Swan (Dugan)

Little Swan (Northwood)

Lords and Ladies

Little Swan (Dugan)

Slightly larger than the Northwood swan shown below, the Dugan version came along in 1909, and can be found in white, green, and blue opalescent glass and various carnival glass colors. The Fenton Company also made a version, but the breast feathering is quite different from the two versions here — more like flower petals than feathers.

Little Swan (Northwood)

Virtually the same design as the Dugan Little Swan, the Northwood version came first and is slightly smaller. It can be found in blue and white (green may be a possibility but I've only seen Dugan ones in that color). Some examples have been gilded on the head and along the rim of the opening and down the tail.

Lords and Ladies

Shown is the previously unreported 7¼" plate in this Davison pattern from England. The Rd number for this pattern is 285312 and previously reported shapes are a small 2¼" salt, a covered butterdish, and a small 3" creamer. The colors are primarily canary opalescent but I have heard of blue on the creamer so I suspect the other pieces were made in this color too. Other shapes probably exist and date of manufacture is 1896.

Lorna

Lorna

Credited first to the Model Flint Glass Company of Albany, Indiana, Northwood nevertheless shows this vase as #562 in a 1900 ad. Obviously, since shards were found in Albany, this vase was copied. At any rate, it is found in white, blue, and canary opalescent glass and stands about 6½" tall.

Lustre Flute

Another Northwood product, Lustre Flute can be found in water sets, table sets, berry sets, custard cups, and vases in opalescent colors of white or blue. The pattern was later made in carnival colors that date to the 1912 era but the vast opalescent production dates to 1907 – 08. Shown is an example with gilt decoration. Lustre Flute is also known as Waffle Band and English Hob Band, but the Lustre Flute title is most widely used.

Lustre Flute

Many Loops

Many Loops was Jefferson's #247 pattern. It is found only on bowls and in the usual opalescent colors of white, blue, and green. The design of overlapping loops, while busy, is very pleasant and reminds one of the child's drawing game Spirograph.

Many Loops

Many Ribs

Maple Leaf

Maple Leaf Chalice

*M*any Ribs

This very distinctive vase with a columnal base was made by the Model Flint Glass Company of Albany, Indiana, in 1902. It can be found in white, blue, and the very attractive canary. This particular vase measures nearly 8" and has the typical slightly flared top.

*M*aple Leaf

Apparently first a Northwood pattern (at least in custard glass), the opalescent items and later carnival glass production were definitely Dugan products. The opalescent glass dates from 1908 – 10. Colors in this glass are green (scarce), white, and blue with a very rare example in vaseline. The only shape reported in opalescent glass seems to be the jelly compote, but others may certainly exist.

*M*aple Leaf Chalice

Another one of the naturalistic pieces from the Northwood Company made in purple slag, as well as opalescent glass. This very pretty vase dates from the 1903 – 05 era. Opalescent colors are white, blue, green, and vaseline. The design is much like Leaf Chalice, also from Northwood and the two are often confused.

Markham Swirl Band with Opal Cobweb

What a name! Actually there are other Markham Swirl designs with various opal designs in white, blue, cranberry, and possibly canary. The example shown is a finger lamp but examples in standard oil lamps are also known.

Markham Swirl Band with Opal Cobweb

Mary Ann

While this vase is well known to carnival glass collectors, it comes as a surprise to many who collect opalescent glass. It came from the Dugan Company, and received its name from the sister of Thomas E.A. and Alfred Dugan (Fanny Mary Ann Dugan). In carnival, the vase is known in an eight scallop and ten scallop top and a three handled, flat topped example called a loving cup. Carnival colors are marigold, amethyst, and a lighter lavender shade. There is also an amber glass example in satin finish. In opalescent glass, the only colors reported are white and blue and both are considered rare.

Mary Ann

May Basket

Still another Jefferson pattern, dating from 1906, this very attractive handled basket was their #87. It can be found in white, blue, and green opalescent glass. Interestingly enough, it has the exact same design as the Northwood Pump and Trough! Since Northwood production of this novelty set predates the Jefferson basket, the mind has to flinch at the obvious pirating that must have gone on. A rare vaseline is known.

May Basket

81

Meander

Melon Optic Swirl (Jefferson)

Melon Swirl

*M*eander

Originally a Jefferson pattern (#233), the moulds were obtained by the Northwood Company after its move to the Wheeling location. The opalescent pieces in white, blue, and green are attributed to Jefferson, and the carnival bowls with Three Fruits Medallion as an interior pattern are strictly Northwood.

*M*elon Optic Swirl (Jefferson)

This very beautiful, tightly crimped bowl has a melon rib exterior that has been shaped into a swirl with a cranberry edging. This bowl appears to be quite close to a series of pieces shown in a 1902 Jefferson ad, showing Stripe, Swirl, and Coindot items. The ad lists colors of white, blue, green, yellow (vaseline), and cranberry.

*M*elon Swirl

Having done a great deal of research and soul-searching, I'm convinced this very beautiful water set may well be from the Indiana, PA, plant at the time of early Dugan production. Examples of handles just like the one on the water set shown are found in 1904 ads showing decorated sets. In addition, the enamel work is so very similar to that found on several Dugan sets made between 1900 and 1905. These sets, more elaborate than most in this enameling, are consistent with Melon Swirl. I certainly hope someone out there can shed more light on this fantastic pattern. It is one of the prettiest I've ever seen.

Milky Way

To opalescent glass collectors this very rare Millersburg item (their only pattern in opalescent glass) is known as Milky Way, but to carnival glass collectors and especially those who collect Millersburg glass, this is a pattern known as Country Kitchen Variant. The only shape known is the bowl and the example shown has been pulled into a square shape that measures 4" x 6".

Monkey (Under a Tree)

Dating to the 1880s, this pattern found mostly in crystal, occasionally turns up in white opalescent glass. Shapes known are water sets, a finger bowl, a toothpick holder, a mug, a pickle jar, a jam jar, a celery vase, and an ashtray; but not all shapes have been found in anything but crystal. Opalescent pieces are very collectible and expensive.

National Swirl

While I haven't seen this opalescent pattern shown in National ads, a 1900 ad from a G. Sommers and Company catalog does show a very similarly shaped pitcher in a decorated design. Please note the reed handle; the ad had three pitchers with reeded handles, indicating the National designation might indeed be right. Colors listed in the catalog were crystal, blue, and green but ruby was also made and perhaps the opalescent pieces evolved from these earlier models.

Milky Way

Monkey (Under a Tree)

National Swirl

Nesting Robins

Netted Roses

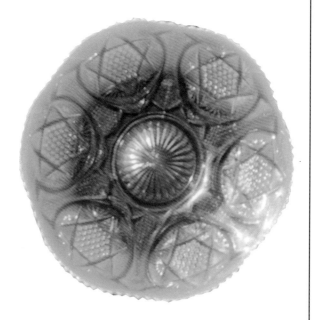

Northern Star

Nesting Robins

Similar in design to the Trout bowl shown elsewhere, this very beautiful 10" bowl is known to come from France and is so marked, with the additional marking: "EZAN." Both designs are of superior workmanship and appear to be about the same age. White is the only opalescent color reported for either.

Netted Roses

Made by the Northwood Company in 1906, this bowl pattern is another of those with one name for opalescent glass and another for carnival. In carnival, the pattern is called Bullseye and Leaves, and is an exterior pattern also. In opalescent glass as Netted Roses, the colors are blue, green, and white, often with a goofus treatment.

Northern Star

Another Fenton pattern, dating to 1908, this very nice geometric is most often found in carnival glass or crystal, but can rarely be found in large plates in white, blue, or green opalescent glass. Just why the small bowls and plates were not made in opalescent treatment is a mystery since 5" bowls, 7" plates, and 11" plates are all known in crystal.

*Northwood Basket
(Bushel Basket)*

Northwood Basket
(Bushel Basket)

Sometimes trademarked, this Northwood novelty was made in limited amounts of opalescent glass in 1905 in white, vaseline, or blue. It was later made in large amounts of custard and carnival glass in many colors and even some shaping variations. The scarce blue opalescent example shown is marked and bears traces of gold paint in the creases of the handle design.

Northwood Block

While I bow to tradition with the name of this pattern, I loudly declare "I do not for one minute believe this is a Northwood pattern!" As you can see by the example shown, the top has the cranberry fritting that was so widely used by the Jefferson Glass Company, and as I said elsewhere in this book, I'm convinced all or nearly all of these pieces with this cranberry treatment are Jefferson. Having said that, the colors available for this Block pattern are white, blue, green, and canary. The only shapes are from one mould; either vase shapes or flattened into footed bowls. This pattern dates from 1905 – 09.

Northwood Block

Northwood Hobnail
(Elson Dew Drop)

While this is the name most used, this particular hobnail pattern was *not* made by Northwood and should be called Elson Dew Drop. It was made in 1887 in colors, crystal, and satin colors (blue and amber), as well as white opalescent glass. In 1893 the Elson firm was reorganized as West Virginia Glass. Dew Drop was listed as their #90 pattern and was not continued after this reorganization.

Northwood Hobnail (Elson Dew Drop)

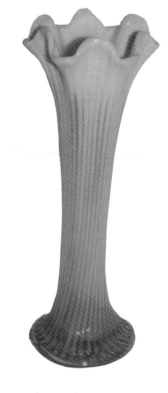

Northwood's Many Ribs

Northwood/Dugan Stripe

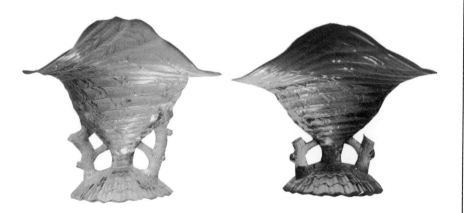

Ocean Shell

Northwood's Many Ribs

Unlike the Model Flint Glass example with this name, the base of the Northwood pattern is not columnated and the design just rolls to an even finish above the straight base. Colors are white, blue, green, and vaseline, and the vases range from 9" to 13" in size.

Northwood/Dugan Stripe

I'm told this vase came from the Indiana, PA, plant where both Northwood and Dugan/Diamond items in opalescent glass were made. As you can see, it is a very pretty canary stripe and is shaped much like a vase in striped opalescent glass in an 1899 Northwood ad in a Butler Brothers catalog. I imagine it was produced in both white and blue also. It is about 7½" tall, with a collar base.

Ocean Shell

Still another of the naturalistic compotes with twig-like supports for stems, Ocean Shell has three variations of these. Some go all the way to the bowl, others are short and are not connected, while still others are longer but remain unattached at the top. Ocean Shell was made by Northwood Company, circa 1904. Opalescent colors are white, blue, and green, and purple slag glass is also known.

Old Man Winter

Old Man Winter

Shown in the two sizes made (the larger one is footed), this pattern came from the Jefferson Company and was advertised as their #135 (small) and #91 (large). Some are marked "Patent 1906" and "Patent March 18, 1902." I've seen the baskets in white, blue, vaseline, and green, but only in green, white, and blue in the larger size. The very interesting handle treatment is a design giveaway and harkens back to Victorian baskets with decorative handles.

Opal Open (Beaded Panels)

Carnival glass collectors have long known this pattern as Beaded Panels. Opalescent glass collectors call it Opal Open. It is shown in a Northwood ad in 1899, so we know they made it. But it later shows up in Dugan ads after 1907, and we know the iridized items are Dugan. To add to the complication, Westmoreland made a reproduction in the 1940s and 1950s that has a solid stem rather than pierced like the originals. Old pieces in opalescent glass were made in white, green, blue, and canary.

Opal Open (Beaded Panels)

Opal Urn Vase

This attractive vase is 7½" tall and has a 2½" base. It is obviously one of the opal stripe patterns but the shape is quite different and earns it this name. I suspect it may be British and can probably be found in white, blue, and canary. Please note the opal stripes end above the plain flare above the base.

Opal Urn Vase

Open Edge Basketweave Base

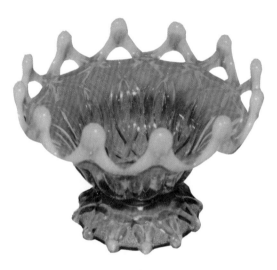

Open O's

Optic Basket

*O*pen Edge Basketweave Base

Introduced into the Fenton line in 1910, this novelty item has been a part of Fenton's production throughout the years, being made in opalescent glass, carnival glass, stretch glass, milk glass, opaque, and all sorts of clear colors. Shapes are bowls of three sizes, plates, candle holders, and vase whimsies. Carnival items sometimes have interior patterns. Early opalescent production colors are white, blue, green, and canary, but later production offered cobalt or royal blue and emerald green. These later examples date to the 1930s.

*O*pen O's

Advertised by Northwood as early as 1903, this very unusual pattern is known mostly in short, squat vase shapes, but it was also made in novelty bowls and a handled ring bowl. Colors are white, blue, green, and canary. It is possible Dugan continued production of this pattern once Northwood moved to Wheeling but, I can't confirm this at this time. The ring bowl is known as Heart Handled Open O's.

*O*ptic Basket

Mould blown, this basket has a ten-panel interior optic pattern, six crimped ruffles, and a twisted vaseline handle that is one piece of glass doubled. It measures 5" tall, 5½" across with a base diameter of 3". The glass is quite thin and there is a pontil mark. I suspect this to be from an English glassmaker.

O ptic Panel

This beautiful vase is truly a work of art with its applied cranberry edging. It is 6" tall with a 2¾" foot. It is mould blown and has eight optic panels that run from the applied base to the top. Coloring is a super vaseline but I feel confident it was made in other colors. I believe this pattern dates to the 1890s and may well be British.

O range Tree

I was very surprised to see this well-known Fenton pattern showing up in the mug. It is very much like the Wild Daffodil mug shown elsewhere in that it has a custard-like opaqueness with a good deal of opalescence. Needless to say, it is a real rarity and one can only speculate if other shapes in this pattern were made in opalescent glass since both bowls and plates are found in carnival glass with opalescent edges.

O ver-All Hobnail

First credited to Nickel Plate Glass, there is some reason to believe production continued once U.S. Glass acquired the plant in 1892. The Over-All Hobnail can be identified on most shapes by the small feet (tumblers are an exception). Colors are white, blue, and canary in opalescent glass, and amber, blue, and clear in crystal. Shapes known in opalescent glass are water sets, table sets, berry sets, (sometimes triangular in shape), celery vase, toothpick holder, finger bowls, and mugs.

Optic Panel

Orange Tree

Over-All Hobnail

Overlapping Leaves (Leaf Tiers)

Palisades (Lined Lattice)

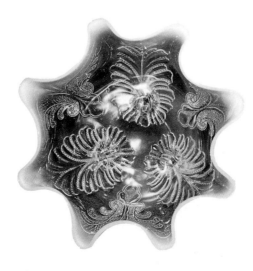

Palm and Scroll

Overlapping Leaves (Leaf Tiers)

While it has been reported as a Northwood product, this pattern has long been known by carnival glass collectors as a Fenton pattern called Leaf Tiers. In opalescent glass the colors are white, blue, and green, but amethyst is a strong possibility. Shapes are the rose bowl (shown), a bowl, and a plate, all footed and from the same mould.

Palisades (Lined Lattice)

Here is yet another pattern first credited to the Northwood Company but known to be a Dugan/Diamond product. Carnival glass collectors call this pattern Lined Lattice, where it can be found in stretched vases and even a light shade for a table lamp called the Princess Lamp. Colors in opalescent glass are white, blue, green, and canary. Vase and novelty bowls are from the same mould.

Palm and Scroll

Credited to the Northwood Company in 1905, Palm and Scroll is actually a product of the Dugan Glass Company and was produced in opalescent glass beginning in 1906, in blue, green, and white. Shapes are various bowls on feet and a neat rose bowl from the same mould. The design is easily recognized; three palm leaves over the curled and ribbed feet and three very artistic feather scrolls between these designs.

Palm Beach

Palm Beach

Made by the U.S. Glass Company, Palm Beach was originally their #15119 and can be found in a wide variety of shapes in both carnival glass and opalescent glass. In the latter, shapes known are water sets, table sets, berry sets, a jelly compote, and a large sauce dish or finger bowl. Colors are blue, white, and canary, with the latter having very strong coloring. Palm Beach dates from 1906, and was continued in production in other forms of glass treatment for several years.

Palm Rosette

I've searched high and low for this beautiful 9" plate pattern without any success, so I've given it a name. If anyone knows more about this pattern, please contact me. I suspect it may be British. The overall design is very satisfying, with cosmos and leaves, palm or fern branches, blooms, and circles of dots. Just about all available space is filled but the design doesn't look busy. I believe this pattern may have been made in blue and vaseline opalescent class as well as white but can't verify this.

Panelled Holly

Found in water sets, table sets, berry sets, novelty bowl shapes, and salt shakers, this pattern comes from the Northwood Glass Company and dates to 1904. Most pieces are considered rare and the only colors in opalescent glass are white and blue. The pattern was also made in limited amounts in carnival glass and crystal that is often decorated and in green decorated glass.

Palm Rosette

Panelled Holly

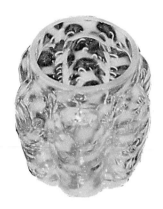

Panelled Sprig

Peacocks (on the Fence)

Peacock Tail

*Opalescent
Glass,
1880 – 1930*

Panelled Sprig

Made by Northwood and perhaps later by Dugan, this pattern dates to 1894, and is found in white opalescent glass only. Shapes known are a cruet, toothpick holder, and salt shakers. Colors were made however, in non-opalescent glass in table sets, water sets, berry sets, and table accessories in both cranberry and rubina but these have been widely reproduced.

Peacocks (on the Fence)

Perhaps one of Northwood's best known patterns, especially in carnival glass, Peacocks on the Fence is found only on bowls or plates. Besides opalescent glass and carnival, a rare example of opaque or marbleized glass that was iridized is well known. The pattern dates from 1908 and in opalescent glass can be found in white, blue, and cobalt. (I suspect canary will eventually show up.) All these opalescent colors are quite scarce as small amounts must have been made.

Peacock Tail

While a casual glance may mistake this rare tumbler for the pressed Drapery, this Fenton tumbler is quite different. Note the octagon base and design that ends about ¾" below the lip. Just why the Fenton Company decided to make this one item in opalescent glass is a mystery since many shapes are known in carnival (but no tumbler!). I have seen a white opalescent example also and certainly green is a strong possibility.

Pearls and Scales

Pearls and Scales

This pattern is credited to the Northwood Company, made in 1905 or 1906. It has been seen in a compote and a stemmed rose bowl from the same mould. Colors are white, blue, green, vaseline, and emerald. Sometimes, a cranberry edging is present, indicating this treatment wasn't exclusively Jefferson's.

Pearl Flowers

Since this pattern is shown in Northwood ads as early as 1904, the maker of this very pretty pattern isn't hard to discern. It is found in bowls of all shapes, rose bowls and nut bowls, all footed and all from the same mould. Colors are white, blue, and green in opalescent glass. It has been reported in carnival glass but I have not seen it in my long years of carnival research and writing.

Pearl Flowers

Piasa Bird

I must confess I am quite skeptical about the origin of this unusual pattern. It has many characteristics of English glass, but some trails lead toward American origin, namely Beaumont. It can be found in both white and blue opalescent glass and the shapes, all from a single mould, are rose bowls, a pulled vase shape, and a spittoon whimsey. All shapes are footed, and the feet remind me somewhat of those on the Inverted Fan and Feather pieces.

Piasa Bird

Plain Jane

Plain Panel

Poinsettia

Plain Jane

I'm relatively sure this pattern came from the Dugan Company; this assumption is based on shape, color, and similarity to other Dugan pieces, chiefly nappies that are shaped the same. Over the years I've seen several Dugan Leaf Ray nappies with exactly the same shaping. Shown is the Plain Jane nappy in blue, but white and green were made. Production was most likely in the 1906 – 09 period.

Plain Panel

While I haven't heard of this vase with the Northwood trademark, I'm sure it was made by that company and the base design is the same as their Feathers vase. Production dates to 1908 or 1909 and colors reported are white, green, and blue, but I wouldn't rule out vaseline. The chief design is the six rib panels that are seperated by wide spaces. These panels run from near the base to the top edge and form a distinctive top flame design. Sizes range from 9" to 14"

Poinsettia

Found mainly on water sets but also known on syrups, bowls, and sugar shakers, this Northwood pattern is also known as Big Daisy. The pitcher shapes vary from a semi-cannonball type to three other tankard styles, and even a ring-necked one. Poinsettia dates from 1902, and can be found in white, cranberry, blue, green, and rarely canary. The tumblers are found in both pressed and blown examples and the bowl, which was made for use in a bride's basket, is most often found without a metal frame. Both the shaker and syrup are quite rare in any color and the tall tankard pitchers are very desirable.

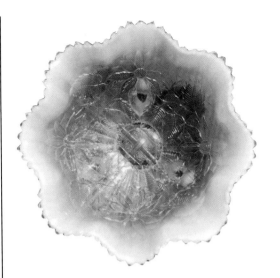

Poinsettia Lattice

Poinsettia Lattice

Made by Northwood Glass, this very beautiful bowl pattern is known in carnival circles as Lattice and Poinsettia, where it is a somewhat rare and very prized pattern. In opalescent glass the colors are limited to white, blue, and vaseline. Production at the Northwood factory dates to 1907, and the latticework is exactly like that of a sister pattern called Cherry Lattice that followed a few years later in other types of glass.

Popsicle Sticks

Credited to the Jefferson Glass Company, this is their #263 pattern. In design it is a simple series of wideunstippled rays that fan out from the center of the bowl shape. Colors are white, blue, and green opalescent glass, and it is found on large bowl shapes with a pedestal base. Shapes may be widely varied including ruffled edges, a banana bowl shape, and even a squared shape.

Pressed Coinspot (#617)

First shown in a 1901 National Glass catalog, this compote (advertised as a card tray) was continued as a Dugan pattern, showing up in their ad for an Oriental assortment, labeled #617. In the vase shape, it later became known as Concave Columns and in carnival glass it is simply called Coinspot. Shapes from the same mould are tall vases, compotes, goblets, and a stemmed banana boat shape. Colors in opalescent glass are white, blue, green, and canary.

Popsicle Sticks

Pressed Coinspot (#617)

Prince Albert and Victoria

Prince William

Princess Diana

Prince Albert and Victoria

Most of the British production of opalescent glass dates from the late 1800s and was made by mostly three manufacturers: Sowerby & Company, Gateshead, England; George Davison & Company, Gateshead-on-Tyne; and Greener & Company of Sunderland, England. Shown is a very attractive creamer in a pattern called Prince Albert and Victoria. It is also known in an open sugar on a stem that looks like a small compote. Colors are blue and canary. This example was made by Davison.

Prince William

Shown is the breakfast set or the open sugar and creamer, made by Davison. Covered sugars were just not part of English glass production. This very attractive pattern can also be found in a beautiful oval plate and water set. Colors, as with most English opalescent glass production, are blue and canary.

Princess Diana

Here is another example of fine British opalescent production by Davison. Princess Diana is a pattern that can be found in many shapes, including a crimped plate, covered butter dish, open sugar, creamer, a water set, a matching tray for the water set, a biscuit set (jam jar with lid and matching plate), salad bowl, novelty bowls, and a compote with a fancy metal base. Colors are the usual blue and canary.

*P*ulled Loop

Well-known to the collectors of carnival glass, Pulled Loop is one of those very scarce Dugan patterns that was made in limited amounts in 1906, in opalescent glass. There are at least two sizes; I've seen 3" and 5" base diameters on these vases. The colors are white, green, and blue with many more green examples available than the other colors. There are six rows of "loop" columns and six rows of ribs that separate them.

*P*ump and Trough

Shown in a 1900 Pitkin and Brooks catalog, along with other Northwood Glass Company items, the very interesting Pump and Trough are listed as #566 and #567 respectively. Colors listed are white, blue, and canary. The design of these items typifies the trend toward naturalism in so many Northwood glass products (Grapevine Clusters, Ocean Shell, Leaf Chalice, and even the Dolphin compote), a trend that continued into their carnival production to some degree with the famous Town Pump. Of course, as with many good things, the Pump and Trough has been widely reproduced, so beware of pumps with flat tops!

*Q*uestion Marks

It is difficult to use only one name for this well-known Dugan pattern for it actually is not one but three patterns. The interior is called Question Marks, the exterior pattern is known as Georgia Belle, and the stem has a Dugan pattern called Puzzle! These compotes are mostly known in carnival glass, but here is the very rare example in a beautiful blue opalescent glass. I suspect it may have been made in white opalescent also, but no examples have been verified at this time; reproduced in vaseline.

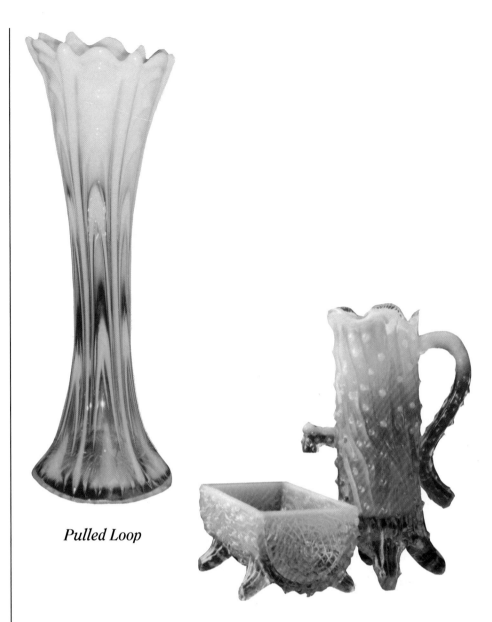

Pulled Loop

Pump and Trough

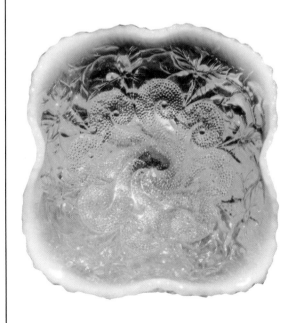

Question Marks

Quilted Daisy Fairy Lamp

Ray

Rayed Heart

*Q*uilted Daisy Fairy Lamp

Anyone who doesn't appreciate this beauty just doesn't like opalescent glass. It is English, I'm sure, and has a super canary color. The base is hard to see since it is a plain color without any milky finish. The design is one of diamonds bordered by sections of daisy filler with a skirt of points below a similar band of points. I believe this piece dates to the 1890s and was probably made in white and blue, as well as, canary.

*R*ay

While this is the only name I've seen this pattern called, the flaring above the base that sets off the ribs could have called for a little more thought. It measures 13" tall with a 3½" base. Colors I've heard about are white, blue, and green, but certainly others may exist.

*R*ayed Heart

Often credited to the Dominion Glass Company of Canada, the opalescent pieces certainly came from Jefferson Glass in this country before the moulds traveled north. Dating from 1910, this pretty compote came in blue, green, and white in opalescent glass and can be found in crystal also, probably Canadian. I know of no other shapes or colors.

Rayed Jane

Exactly like the Plain Jane stemmed nappy shown elsewhere, except this one has scalloped edges and interior rays. This nappy is another Dugan/Diamond piece. Just why a glass company would make two such similar pieces has always been a mystery but both are quite attractive. The Rayed Jane nappy comes in the 1909 – 1914 era and was made in white and green opalescent too.

Reflecting Diamonds

Let me say again, while they were both Dugan patterns, Reflecting Diamonds is not the same pattern as Compass. Having said that, please note Reflecting Diamonds appears in bowl shapes only and has been found as early as 1905, in Butler Brothers ads featuring Dugan/Diamond patterns. Like so many geometric patterns, this one has a series of diamonds filled with a file pattern bordered by fan shapes standing back-to-back between the diamonds. The base has the exact overlapping star design as that found on the Compass base.

Regal

This pattern is certainly rightly named for it has a regal look. It was made by the Northwood Company in 1905, and some pieces are marked. Regal can be found in table sets, water sets, berry sets, salt shakers, and cruets in white, green, and blue opalescent glass as well as in crystal and emerald green glass with gilding. The pattern was also known as Blocked Midriff but the Regal name is most widely used.

Rayed Jane

Reflecting Diamonds

Regal

Reverse Drapery

Reverse Drapery

Shown is the bowl in this well-known Fenton pattern but it was also pulled into a vase that is often confused with the similar Boggy Bayou pattern also from the Fenton company. In carnival glass, the Reverse Drapery pattern is called Cut Arcs further adding to the confusion. Opalescent colors in Reverse Drapery are white, blue, green, and amethyst. An occasional plate can be found also.

Reverse Swirl

Made by the Buckeye Glass Company of Martin's Ferry, Ohio, and later in some degree by the Model Flint Glass Company of Albany, Indiana, this beautiful pattern dates from 1888. The lamp shown is from Buckeye and was made in two sizes. It is considered quite rare. Other shapes found are water sets, cruet, table sets, berry sets, salt shakers, syrups, sugar shaker, custard cup, mustard pot, toothpick holder, night lamps, a finger bowl, water bottles in two sizes, a caster set (four pieces in metal holder), and a very scarce tall salt shaker. Colors are white, blue, canary, and cranberry, and occasionally some items are satin finished.

Rib and Big Thumbprints

This Dugan/Diamond vase is shown in Butler Brothers ads from fall 1906 along with several Dugan patterns so we know who made this rather undistinguished pattern. The design, four ribs in five columns with spots of opalescence between, is hard to see except on the unswung examples.

Reverse Swirl

Rib and Big Thumbprints

Rib Optic

*R*ib Optic

The Fenton Company made this pattern in 1927 in the bedroom set or tumble-up (the tumbler is missing) in green, vaseline, blue, and the light cranberry shown. The water bottle is 6" tall and has a base diameter of 3½".

*R*ibbed (Opal) Lattice

This is probably a Northwood Glass pattern, but may have been an earlier LaBelle Glass product. It is found in water sets, a cruet, salt shakers, syrup, table set, berry set, toothpick holder, sugar shakers in two sizes, and a celery vase. Colors are white, blue, and cranberry.

*R*ibbed Spiral

Made by the Model Flint Glass Company of Albany, Indiana, in 1902, this pattern can be found in a host of shapes including table sets, water sets, berry sets, plates, cups and saucers, toothpick holder, salt shaker, jelly compote, various bowls, and vases of all sizes. Colors are white, blue, and canary.

Ribbed (Opal) Lattice

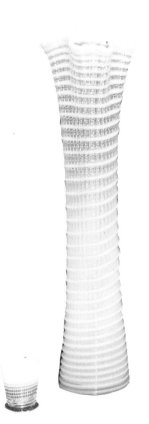

Ribbed Spiral

Richelieu

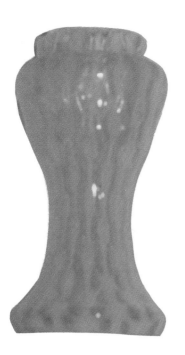

Ric-Rac

Ring Handled Basket

Richelieu

Another of those very attractive British patterns, this one is from Davison and Company and dates to 1885. The RD number of this pattern is #96945 and items made are a jelly compote, creamer, divided dish, cracker jar, handled basket, various bowl shapes, and a neat handled nappy. Colors are white, blue, and canary. Shown is a basket shape.

Ric-Rac

Missing its lid, this unusual blown jar in vaseline stands 8¼" tall and has a pontil mark on the base. The glass is very thin and I suspect it is English. If anyone knows it by another name, I'd be interested in hearing from them. It may well have been made in other colors including white and blue.

Ring Handled Basket

As I've said before, I really think this is just another shape in Opal Open (or Beaded Panels as it is also known). At any rate, I will show it alone in the handled basket or handled center bowl shape. It is also found on salt shakers as well as the compote called Opal Open. Colors are blue and white, sometimes with a clambroth effect. This coloring can be clearly seen in the ring just below the handle on the piece shown. This piece measures 7½" wide.

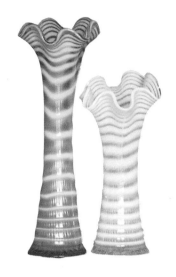

Ripple

Ripple

I must apologize to all the collectors I've told this vase didn't exist and their vases had to be Ribbed Spiral ones. These scarce Ripple vases, made by Imperial, have a many rayed base and are more flared at the top. Colors reported so far are blue, vaseline, and green, but surely white was also made. Of course, this was a very popular carnival glass design, made in at least four base diameters and many carnival colors.

Rococo

While this very pretty blown pattern resembles both Arabian Nights and Alhambra, it is slightly different than either. The piece shown is a ruffled square bowl, intended for a bride's basket, and probably dates in the 1890 to 1910 era. Since the other two patterns can be found in white, blue, canary, and cranberry, I'd bet Rococo can be found in these opalescent colors also.

Rose Show

Known primarily as a carnival glass pattern, this very beautiful bowl can also be found in limited amounts in white and blue opalescent glass. Reputed to be a Northwood pattern, the bowl has a reverse pattern of Woven Wonder, a spin-off design of Frosted Leaf and Basketweave.

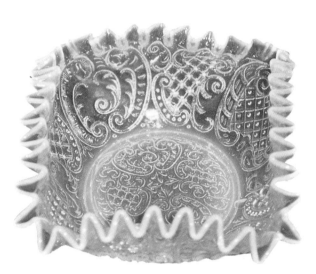

Rococo

Rose Show

103

Rose Spatter

Rose Spray

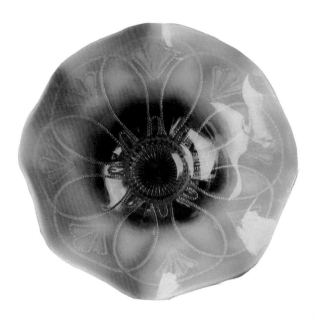

R ose Spatter

I am told by a reputable dealer and researcher that this very attractive pitcher with a ball shape came from either the Beaumont Glass Company or the Buckeye Company (both of Martins Ferry, Ohio). I haven't been able to verify either as the maker at this time. The coloring is much like the finish found on Northwood's Leaf Mold items called "tortoise shell spatter." At any rate, it's a super pitcher, and I believe it dates to the 1890s.

R ose Spray

Found mostly in carnival glass, this Fenton compote can also be seen on rare occasions on opalescent glass. Colors are white (French), blue, or amethyst, and all are scarce. Production dates from 1910 to 1914. The design of a stem, leaves, and a rose is little more than a line drawing and is very hard to see.

R oulette

Shown in a 1906 ad from a Lyon Brothers catalog, this Northwood pattern is very similar to the Diamond Point and Fleur-de-Lis pattern shown elsewhere. Many shapings were made from the bowl mould including a rose bowl, ruffled and flared bowls, and even a plate in white, blue, and green.

Roulette

Royal Scandal

What a beautiful piece of glass work this British wall pocket vase is! It is very likely a product of Davison, minus the typical English RD number and measures some 6" in length. I've seen it in a beautiful blue opalescent as well as the canary one shown. The design seems to be a series of rope-like strips that cross over shell-type ribbing. At each side is a large petaled flower and the hanging band looks like thorny branches. The mould work and opalescence are simply outstanding. As far as I know, there is no known name for the pattern, so I've taken the liberty of providing a name; if I'm mistaken, I'll soon hear about it.

Rubena Verde

These beautiful Jack-in-the-Pulpit vases from Hobbs, Brockunier of Wheeling date to the 1880s and are a prime example of a ware known as Rubena Verde. These items are blown, shading from vaseline to cranberry with opalescence on the reverse of the throat. They stand 6 ½" tall and are 5 ¼" wide, approximately. This is art glass at its best, typical of what was being made a century ago.

Ruffles and Rings

Originally another of the Jefferson Glass patterns that came into the Northwood production orbit, the opalescent version appears to have been made in 1906 and after. In carnival glass, the pattern has been found as an exterior one with such designs as Rosette, and even on a rare flint opalescent bowl with no interior pattern, marigold iridizing, and an added floral border edging. Colors in opalescent glass are white, blue, and green.

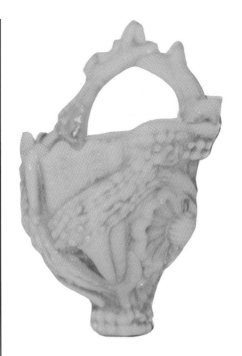

Royal Scandal

Rubena Verde

Ruffles and Rings

Ruffles and Rings with Daisy Band

Ruffles and Rings with Daisy Band

Just why the Northwood Company decided to do this variant of the Ruffles and Rings pattern is a mystery, but here they've added a classy banding of daisies along the outer edge. Since both Jefferson and Northwood are credited with Ruffles and Rings, perhaps the regular is Jefferson's that was later made by Northwood who then added the band. At any rate, Northwood later made both versions in carnival glass and a very rare example of marigold with an opalescent daisy band exists. Opalescent colors are the usual white, blue, and green.

S-Repeat (National)

First advertised in a Butler Brothers ad of glass from the newly formed Dugan Glass Company, S-Repeat (or National as it was then called) seems to be a pattern designed while the plant was still operated by Northwood as a part of National Glass, but only released once Dugan had taken over. The ad dates to May, 1903. In opalescent glass, the colors made were white, blue, and green in limited amounts. Additional types of glass, including crystal, apple green, blue, and amethyst, were decorated and made in a wide range of shapes. In opalescent glass, shapes known are table sets, water sets, and berry sets. In addition, the goblet has now been found in blue opalescent (shown elsewhere in this book) formed into a compote shape with the Constellation pattern added to the interior.

S-Repeat (National)

Scheherezade

Scheherezade

While the maker of this very pretty pattern has not been confirmed, I really believe we need look no further than the Dugan/Diamond Company. Found primarily in bowls, the opalescent colors are white, blue, and green. The design of file triangles, finecut triangles, and hobstars is a close cousin to Dugan's Reflecting Diamonds, but has more than enough difference to tell it from any other pattern. Scheherezade is a rather scarce pattern, but well worth looking for.

Scroll with Acanthus

Credited to the Northwood Company, Scroll with Acanthus can be found in water sets, table sets, berry sets, a jelly compote, salt shaker, toothpick holder, and cruet. Colors are white, blue, and canary opalescent glass with some novelties in green opalescent, crystal, and purple slag, as well as decorated green and blue crystal. Production dates from 1903.

Scroll with Acanthus

Sea Scroll

I've spent days trying to learn the name and origin of this nice compote (I'm convinced it is British) with no luck so I've chosen this name. The design is a series of scrolls around the base of the compote's bowl. The stem has a ring near the top and one near the base. The compote measures 4¾" tall, 5¼" across the top and has a 2⅝" base. Please let me know if anyone has more information about this fine pattern.

Sea Scroll

Sea Spray

Seaweed

Shell (Beaded Shell)

Sea Spray

Made by the Jefferson Glass Company in 1906 – 07, this was their #192 pattern. The only shape reported is the very attractive nappy and the colors are the usual white, green, and blue opalescent. The design is somewhat similar to the S-Repeat but has an interesting beading added below the "S" and sections of line filler above.

Seaweed

First made by Hobbs, Brockunier in water sets, a salt shaker, a syrup, table sets, berry sets, a barber bottle, a sugar shaker, a pickle caster, a cruet, and two sizes of oil bottle, this pattern has become confused with a pattern called Coral Reef. The differences lie in the shaping of the small bulb and line patterns and if you will make a comparison of both you will be able to instantly tell them apart. Hobbs made both patterns and Coral Reef was also made by Beaumont and possibly Northwood a few years after the Hobbs production. Colors in Seaweed are white, blue, and cranberry.

Shell (Beaded Shell)

While this Dugan pattern is known as Shell in opalescent glass, collectors of carnival and other types of glass recognize it as the Beaded Shell pattern. It was made in 1905, in a host of shapes including water sets, berry sets, cruet, toothpick holder, salt shaker, mug, rare compotes, and cruet set. Colors are white, green, blue, canary, electric blue, and apple green plus carnival colors. Has been reproduced by Mosser.

Shell and Dots

Shell and Dots

Made by the Jefferson Company, Shell and Dots is nothing more than the well-known Beaded Fans pattern with a series of bubble-like dots on the base. Made in 1905, this pattern can be found in white, green, and blue opalescent.

Shell and Wild Rose

Called simply Wild Rose by carnival glass collectors this Northwood pattern dates from 1906. In opalescent glass it was made in white, blue, and green, but was later a part of their iridized production and is quite popular in carnival glass. The open edged inverted heart border is a wonder in glass work and must have been a mould maker's nightmare. A rare vaseline is known.

Shell and Wild Rose

Simple Simon

Carnival glass collectors know this pattern as Graceful. It was a product of the Northwood Company dating from 1908 – 09. In carnival glass, it is made in most Northwood non-pastel colors, but in opalescent glass the colors are limited to green, white, and a scarce blue. While the design isn't too well planned, the compote's shape adds class, and the workmanship is quality.

Simple Simon

Singing Birds

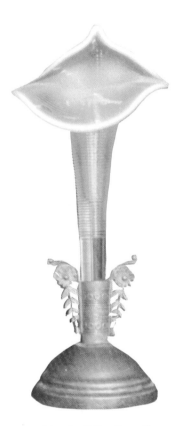

Single Lily Spool

Single Poinsettia

Singing Birds

As I've stated in the first edition of this book, this is a famous Northwood pattern, well known in carnival glass in many shapes and also produced in custard and clear glass with decoration. In opalescent glass, the only shape known until 1995 was the rare mug shape in blue, white, and vaseline advertised in 1907. Now we have found a very rare blue opalescent tumbler whimsey that is shown in the whimsey section of this book, so other pieces may well have been made and will show up in the future.

Single Lily Spool

We now know this pattern is from Jefferson Glass and as I said in the first edition of this book, the metal holder has an Art Deco look. Colors now reported are green, white, and blue and the opalescnce is just fantastic on all I've seen. I believe the holder was made to be used with other lily horns as well as this one and so be alert for what may be out there.

Single Poinsettia

While I haven't learned very much about this previously unreported pattern, all indications gathered from the shape of the bowl, fluting, the design itself, and the plain marie seem to point to the Dugan/Diamond concern as a possible maker. If so, I'm confident the piece was made in other colors, probably blue and green; and it is possible this piece had a goofus treatment at one time. At any rate, it is a rare item and very attractive.

Sir Lancelot

*S*ir Lancelot

Advertised in a Butler Brothers ad in 1906, along with several well-known Northwood patterns, including Shell and Wild Rose, Diamond Point, and Hilltop Vines, Sir Lancelot is now recognized as a Northwood product. The shapes are novelty bowls with a dome base in white, blue, and green opalescent glass. The design, three fleur-de-lis and three starburst figures on a stippled background, is very interesting and quite attractive. The dome base is rayed.

Smooth Rib

*S*mooth Rib

While it looks plain, this 7⅝" bowl on a collar base really has 20 panels of ribbing on the interior. The coloring is vaseline with very good opalescence. The collar base measures 2½" and it is a two mould piece. I'm sure this pattern was made in other colors but I haven't seen them so far, and I haven't a clue as to the maker.

*S*nowflake

Much like its sister pattern, Christmas Snowflake, this Northwood product dates to 1890, and can be found only on oil lamps in three sizes (table size, hand lamps, and night lamps). Colors in opalescent glass are white, blue, and cranberry. Strangely, these lamps were advertised with matching chimneys but few seem to exist. Shown are the table lamp in cranberry and the hand lamp in white.

Snowflake

Spanish Lace

Spatter

Spattered Coinspot

Spanish Lace

Introduced by the Northwood Company to American collectors in 1899, this pattern has been known as Opaline Brocade, as well as its more popular name, Spanish Lace. Shapes made are water sets (three pitcher styles), table sets, cruet, salt shaker, wine decanter (very rare), night lamp, water bottle, perfume bottle, rose bowl, and a celery vase, as well as vases in several sizes. In addition several items are fitted with metal parts including a bride's basket and cracker jar. Colors are white, blue, and cranberry, with limited production of some shapes in green, and a few items in a canary that are likely of an English origin. A handled basket, a cruet, and a rose bowl have recently been made by Fenton in cranberry, but these are the only items that are not old. The pitcher shown is in the Ribbon Tie mould.

Spatter

This treatment was used by both Northwood and Dugan/Diamond on water sets, bowls, and vases but I feel from both the shape and top design this piece is from the latter company. It stands 9" tall and the random opalescent swirling through the glass is quite attractive.

Spattered Coinspot

The shape of this very beautiful pitcher seems to be the same ball shape that Northwood used on the Daisy and Fern pitcher, but certainly it may well belong to another maker. I'm confident it is old, dating from the late 1800s, and as far as desirability is concerned it would have to be quite high. The coloring is simply beautiful with spatters of cranberry mixed with the flecks of white.

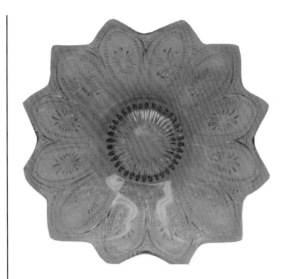

Spokes and Wheels

Spokes and Wheels

Shown in a 1906 Butler Brothers ad along with several other Northwood Company patterns, Spokes and Wheels can be found in a variety of bowl shapes as well as plates that are tri-cornered or square. Colors are the usual white, blue, and green opalescent, but a rare aqua piece in a square plate exists.

Spool of Threads

Primarily a compote pattern, Spool of Threads is a Northwood pattern dating to 1905. It was advertised in 1902 in purple slag, and in opalescent glass it can be found in white, blue, canary, and perhaps green. I have heard of one item flattened out into a stemmed tray but haven't seen it.

Spool of Threads

Squirrel and Acorn

Here is one of the most appealing patterns in opalescent glass and in the whimsey section I show the vase. At this time, I do not know the maker of this pattern but can tell you it is quite rare, especially in blue and white. It was also made in a very scarce green. All shapes, a footed bowl, the compote, and the vase are from the same mould showing six panels with alternating designs of a frisky squirrel, acorn, and leaves. The base has a raised scale-like pattern. I'm sure the pattern dates to the 1904 – 10 era.

Squirrel and Acorn

113

Star Base

Stars and Bars

Stars and Stripes

Star Base

I've searched and searched for this pattern (if one can call it a pattern), but without success so I've taken the liberty of giving it the most obvious name possible. I'd suspect it was made in other colors but haven't seen any. I'd appreciate hearing from anyone who can shed some light on this item.

Stars and Bars

Glass furniture knobs were the first pieces of pressed glass made in this country and had a beginning in the 1820s, so it isn't surprising to see examples of opalescent knobs like the one shown. Today, these are scarce and to find a complete set is next to impossible. The example shown has a series of stars in prisms around the top and rows of bars on the sides. It is but one of many designs known and is found in at least two sizes. Most of these knobs are white but cranberry opalescent is known.

Stars and Stripes

While this pattern has been reproduced by the Fenton Company for the L.G. Wright Company, particularly in tumblers, a pitcher, and a small milk pitcher with reeded handle, the design originally came from Hobbs (1890) and later from Beaumont (1899). Original shapes were water sets, a barber bottle, cruet, finger bowl, and lamp shades. Colors were white, blue, and cranberry opalescent. The Wright reproduction cruets can be found with both ruffled and tri-cornered tops and both have reeded handles. Some of the repro items, especially the new water pitchers in blue, are very poorly done and the matching tumblers are thick and splotchy in coloring.

Stork and Rushes

Stork and Rushes

Found mostly in carnival glass in several shapes, this quite scarce mug and a tumbler are the only known shapes (thus far) in opalescent glass. Colors reported from Dugan Glass Company ads dating from 1909 are white and blue, but certainly green or vaseline may exist. There are two border bands on this pattern but as you can see, the opalescent pieces have the diamond file designed band at the top and bottom. The second banding, a series of dots, seems to appear only on carnival items.

Strawberry

A Fenton pattern that is known by most carnival glass collectors, the only two shapes in opalescent glass seems to be a two-handled bon-bon and a small sauce bowl. The bon-bon has been found in white and the sauce in amethyst opalescent but surely there are other colors out there somewhere. Production is from the 1915 – 1919 period, the same as carnival glass pieces.

Strawberry

Stork and Swan

This very attractive syrup seems most likely to be of English origin. It is white with heavy opalescence from top to bottom. The handle is applied and the piece measures 5½" tall with a base width of 2¾. The metal lid is marked "Patd. Nov. 16th 1869." On one side is a very attractive Swan design featuring cattails and the floating swan, and on the reverse side, a stork (or crane) stands among cattails with a blooming tree on the opposite area. The rest of the piece is filled with vertical ribbing.

Stork and Swan

Stripe

Stripe Condiment Set

Sunburst-on-Shield

Stripe

Made by many glass companies including Northwood, Nickel-Plate, Jefferson, Buckeye, Beaumont, and even English production, Stripe (or Oval Stripe as it is also known) dates from 1886, and continued at one concern or another until 1905. Colors are white, blue, canary, cranberry, and even some rubina opalescent glass. Shapes include water sets with many shapes in pitchers, cruets, salt shakers of several shapes, syrups, finger bowls, sugar shakers, two caster sets, various oil lamps and miniature lamps, lamp shades, vases, celery vases, bowls, toothpick holder, barber bottle, wine decanter, several sizes in tumblers, and shot glasses. Reproductions are well known in the barber bottle, small 5" – 7" pitchers, and perhaps other shapes. I believe the example shown is Nickel-Plate glass.

Stripe Condiment Set

Advertised in an 1889 Butler Brothers ad, this very pretty condiment set consists of a white opalescent base or server, a white mustard pot with metal fittings, a cranberry vinegar (not original stopper), and a pair of salt shakers, one in blue and one in white. As I said earlier, Stripe was made primarily by Hobbs, Brockunier, but later in water sets and other pieces by Northwood. This set is a very desirable collectible and worth looking for.

Sunburst-on-Shield

While I will admit I much prefer the original Northwood name for this pattern (Diadem), I understand most collectors call it Sunburst-on-Shield. It dates to 1905, and in opalescent glass was made in table sets, berry sets, water sets, nappy, bowls, cruet, and the two-piece breakfast set shown. Colors are mostly blue and canary with some shapes in white known. The nappy and cruet are rare and the water set very scarce, as is a celery tray.

Swag with Brackets

Swag with Brackets

Swag with Brackets is a product of the Jefferson Glass Company and dates to 1904. It can be found in white, blue, green, and canary opalescent glass, as well as crystal, amethyst, blue, and green, that are often decorated. Shapes are table sets, water sets, berry sets, toothpick holders, salt shakers, cruets, jelly compotes, and many novelties. Notice the cranberry fritt edging often found on Jefferson items.

Swastika

Shown on the Diamonds and Clubs mould, this Dugan/Diamond opalescent pattern can also be found on a ball-type pitcher mould, as well as on tumblers and a syrup. Colors are white, green, blue, and cranberry. The syrups can be found in both panelled and ball shapes. All pieces date from 1907 production and are quite scarce. It is a shame more shapes weren't developed in this pattern.

Swastika

Swirl

Virtually every glass company who made opalescent glass had a Swirl design, and it is quite difficult to distinguish one maker's examples from the others except by shapes known to have been favored by some companies. It is for this reason I believe this pitcher and tumbler shown came from the Jefferson Glass Company, since it matches the shape of pitchers they made in both Swirling Maze and Lattice. Colors are blue, white, and cranberry, with green and canary strong possibilities. Notice that the handle is not reeded as on the Lattice pitcher in this shape. (The Swirling Maze also has no reeding.)

Swirl

Swirl (Northwood Ball Shape)

Swirling Maze

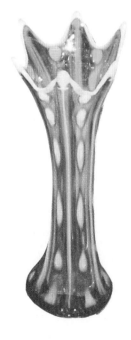

Target

Swirl (Northwood Ball Shape)

Here's another look at one of the many Swirl patterns. This one is on Northwood's ball shape in the water set. This shape was also made by the Dugan Company and dates to (Hobb production) 1890. The Northwood version is sometimes called a variant. Colors are primarily white, blue, and cranberry, although rare examples of canary are known.

Swirling Maze

While the ruffled salad bowls are known to have come from the Jefferson Glass Company (1905), there is some question about who made the various pitchers and tumblers in this pattern. (The pitchers have been found in three shapes.) Colors are white, blue, green, canary, and cranberry. I personally feel all pieces had the same maker and list the water sets as Jefferson also until proven wrong. I would be very surprised if additional shapes weren't made and eventually come to light.

Target

When I first showed this rare vase by the Dugan/Diamond Glass Company only a green example was known. Now both white and blue have been seen and all are equally as rare. The Target pattern is well known by carnival glass collectors where it was made in several colors including peach opalescent.

Thousand Eye

Thousand Eye

First made in 1888 by Richards and Hartley and later by U. S. Glass once they had absorbed the factory in 1892, Thousand Eye can be found in white opalescent, crystal, and several colors in plain crystal. Shapes are numerous and include table sets, berry sets, water sets, compotes, a celery vase, a cruet, shakers, a toothpick holder, bottles of various sizes, novelty bowls, and various compotes.

Thread and Rib

Harry Northwood must have been fascinated with epergnes. He designed the one shown here in 1906. He patented two additional designs, the well-known Wide Panel epergne in 1909 and a universal tube-receiving pedestal apparatus in 1916. The Thread and Rib epergne is shown in a 1906 Northwood catalog as #305 Flower Stand. It measures 18" tall and was available in white, blue, and green opalescent glass, although the example shown is vaseline opalescent and must have been an addition to the line. The base dish measures 12" and has threading below the metal and glass lily fittings. It sold in an assortment of nine for $7.50!

Threaded Grape

Mistakenly called Dugan's Vintage by one writer, this pattern, on a stem, has many differences. First, the grapes and leaves fan out from the center of the bowl rather than circling it. Then there is the band of eight thin threads that circle near the outer edge. And finally, there is a short stem and a dome base that has a teardrop and beading pattern. This Dugan/Diamond product is a super pattern, seldom found, and very desirable. It was made in blue, white, and green opalescent and dates to 1909.

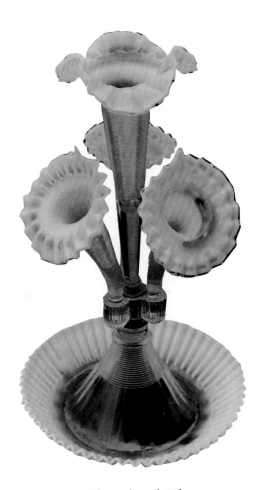

Thread and Rib

Threaded Grape

119

Threaded Optic

Three Fruits

Three Fruits and Meander

Threaded Optic

While I've named this pattern Threaded Optic, it could well be called "Inside Ribbing with Threading" as well. It may well be a spin-off pattern from the well-known Inside Ribbing pattern made by the Beaumont Glass Company of Martins Ferry, Ohio, but it has the look and coloring of a Dugan product. I've only seen the rose bowl in blue opalescent, but it was made in other colors and shapes from the same mould such as bowls, plates, and vases. The ribbing or optic is all interior and the threading or horizontal rings are on the outside. The marie is plain and slightly raised. Also called Band and Rib. Three sizes of bowls are known.

Three Fruits

Dating from 1907, this Northwood pattern is mostly known in carnival glass production, but it was also made in limited amounts in opalescent glass in white and blue. The exterior pattern is called Thin Rib and the interior pattern of cherries, pears, and apples with leaves is an attractive one.

Three Fruits and Meander

In carnival glass this pattern is known as Three Fruits Medallion because of the leaf medallion in the interior's center. The meander pattern is on the exterior and shows through nicely with the pattern of fruits and leaves on the inside. This is a Northwood pattern and is found on both white and blue opalescent glass and many colors of carnival.

Opalescent Glass, 1880 – 1930

Tines

Tiny Tears

Tines

Since I haven't been able to find another name for this beautiful vase (I suspect it may be British in origin), I named it Tines after the fork-like ridges that run vertically on the exterior from top to bottom. It also has a nice interior optic or ribbing. The opalescence is around the neck where the glass color is actually blue instead of the green found on the rest of the vase! This beauty stands 9½" tall and is very graceful indeed. The quality of the glass is very fine.

Tiny Tears

Very little information seems to be available for this vase although it appears to have the same coloring as so many vase patterns from either Northwood or Dugan/Diamond. The example shown stands 14" tall, has a rayed marie with 28 rays and an extended ridge above the base with fine ribbing on the inside, all around the base. I'm sure this was made in the usual opalescent colors and must have come from the 1903 – 10 era of production.

Tokyo

Made by the Jefferson Glass Company, Tokyo is a very distinctive pattern that can be found in table sets, water sets, berry sets, salt shakers, cruet, jelly compote, toothpick holder, vase, and a footed plate. Colors are white, blue, and green in opalescent glass and plain crystal, decorated blue and apple green glass. A few years ago Tokyo was reproduced in some shapes including the compote, so buy with caution.

Tokyo

121

Tree of Love

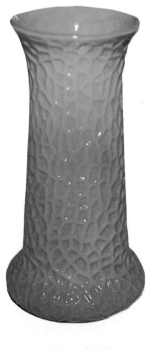

Tree of Life

Tree Stump

Tree of Life

This very unusual vase came as a great surprise to me and made me question my sanity for a moment. I *believe* it may be from Dugan/Diamond since they are known to have made some wall pocket vases and a basket in this pattern. I'd certainly appreciate any information on this vase anyone may offer and I'm confident other colors were made. It stands about 9" tall.

Tree of Love

The maker of this very nice pattern, seen only in white opalescent glass so far, is a mystery, however, I strongly feel it is a British pattern. Shown are two of the shapes known, the compote and the plate. The interior design is one of leaves, stems, and flowers, but the leaves look like hearts! In the base is a series of nine diamonds circled by beading. The stem of the compote looks very unusual with a bolt- and nut-like configuration. I believe the pattern dates to the early 1900s.

Tree Stump

While this very interesting mug shape is usually called just Stump, the formal name is Tree Stump. The mould work is very good as is the coloring and the opalescence. Most collectors feel this item is from the Northwood Company and I agree it certainly has all the attributes of Harry Northwood's quality. In size it is shorter than most mugs and the very realistic tree branch handle and the knots on the bark add real interest. Colors are green, white, and blue opalescent and all are rather scarce.

Opalescent
Glass,
1880 – 1930

*T*ree Trunk

This well-known Northwood vase is sometimes marked and was made in several sizes in carnival glass, including a huge example with an 8" base diameter called an elephant vase. In opalescent glass, I know of only the standard size (3¼" base) that can be stretched from 7" to 14" in height. Opalescent colors are white, green, and blue and date from 1907 – 08. Besides carnival glass and opalescent glass, Tree Trunk can be found in Northwood's Opal (milk glass), Ivory (custard glass), or a rare color called Sorbini, a blue marbled opaque glass with a marigold iridized spray coating.

*T*rellis

This stemmed tumbler stands 4 ½" tall. Aside from that, I can offer very little information. The opalescence forms a diamond quilting and there is an optic effect, but the difference from the Diamond pattern is evident. Origin may be England but I can't be sure. I base this on the heavy opalizing and the general shape.

*T*riangle

There may well be another name for this 4" tall match holder but I haven't heard it. The sides measure 3" across. The pattern relies on the three-corner columns and the bands at top and bottom since the rest of the glass is plain. The entire piece stands on ball feet. Colors are pimarily white or blue, but green or vaseline may well exist. Made by Sowerby of England.

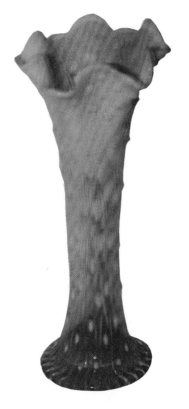

Tree Trunk

Trellis

Triangle

123

Twigs

Twist

Twisted Rib

Twigs

First advertised in 1898 as a Northwood product in opalescent glass, the Twigs pattern was another of those patterns later produced by Dugan/Diamond once Northwood left the Indiana, PA, plant. In opalescent glass, Twigs is found in two sizes (the smaller 5" size and a slightly larger 6¹/₂" example) and is known in blue, white, green, and canary. In carnival glass, Dugan later made the same twig footed vase and a sister vase without twig feet called Beauty Bud Vase. These Dugan vases can be found in marigold, amethyst, peach opalescent, and I recently saw a strange tortoise-shell-over-marigold example that must have been an experimental item.

Twist

As a part of the National Glass Company, Model Flint Glass of Albany, Indiana, produced this very collectible miniature table set consisting of the covered butter, sugar, creamer, and spooner. Colors known are white, blue, and vaseline opalescent, and crystal (plain, frosted, or decorated). A secondary name for this pattern is Ribbed Swirl. The examples shown are a spooner in white and a butter base and sugar base in vaseline.

Twisted Rib

This well-known Dugan/Diamond vase pattern is also known as Spiralex by carnival glass collectors, and was swirled or twisted from the Wide Rib vase shown elsewhere. Production began in about 1906 in crystal, colored glass, opalescent glass, and carnival glass, and continued for several years. Opalescent colors known are white, blue, and green with the latter being the hardest to find. Sizes range from 9" to 13".

*T*wister

Found primarily in bowls in white, green, and blue opalescent, very scarce plates are also known. The maker has not been established, at least to my knowledge, but the base design of a radiating star is much like that found on the Carousel pattern which is known to be a Jefferson Glass product.

*U*niversal Northwood Tumbler

When the Northwood Company produced Alaska and Klondyke (Fluted Scrolls or Jackson), the same tumbler mould was used for both patterns. By adding an enameled design (forget-me-nots for Alaska, daisies for Fluted Scrolls), the company not only saved money but produced similar but distinctive patterns. I am showing one of these tumblers without the enameling to show the design as it came from the mould. Naturally it came in all colors of each pattern and was made in opalescent glass, custard, crystal, and emerald green. In addition to the tumbler, a similar universal salt shaker was produced for these patterns.

*V*enetian Beauty Night Lamp

Shown in an 1890 Butler Brothers ad, this miniature lamp is 3¼" tall. Colors are white, blue, and vaseline opalescent with a rare cranberry reported. This lamp was intended to sell for 25¢ in that age! Wholesale prices were $1.90 a dozen (times have really changed, haven't they?) and an accompanying ad advertised the matching chimney at 84¢ a dozen. The shade on the example shown is not original.

Twister

Universal Northwood Tumbler

Venetian Beauty Night Lamp

Venice

Victoria and Albert

Victorian Hamper

Venice

Shown in the 1888 *American Potter and Illuminator*, this very beautiful table lamp had a matching shade and is said to have been made with either a blue or white opalescent stripe on the fonts. They came in 8", 9", and 10" sizes.

Victoria and Albert

Made by Davison, this English pattern bears the RD #303519, and can be found in table sets as well as a cracker jar. The date of production was 1897, and the colors reported are blue and canary but white was probably made. The piece shown is the open sugar on a stem.

Victorian Hamper

Listed in an 1882 Sowerby pattern book as #1187½, this very pretty little novelty basket measures 5" long and 2½" tall. It has two rope-like handles and a woven pattern that goes from the rope edging to the ground base. The coloring is very soft like so much glass from England and it has good opalescence. It was probably made in canary as well as the advertised crystal (flint), opal, turquoise, Patent Queen's Ware, and Blanc de Lait treatments. Queen's Ware is an opaque glass with yellow tint, similar to custard glass, and Blanc de Lait is milk glass. The hamper was also made in malachite or slag glass.

Victorian Stripe with Flowers

While this is certainly pure art glass like so many items of the 1890s, I felt one piece of decorated glass with applied floral sprays might be in order to set a bit of perspective as to where the opalescent glass craze started before it progressed into the mostly pressed items we show elsewhere. This beautiful 10" vase is likely British and is tissue-paper thin, with stems of applied clear glass and flowers that have a cranberry beading. Notice the flaring base, much like many Northwood tankard pitchers that came later.

Vintage

This exterior pattern on 8" – 9" bowls with dome bases is yet another of those patterns first made by Jefferson in opalescent glass and later at the Northwood plant in Wheeling. The Northwood products in carnival glass usually compliment an interior pattern such as Rosettes or Three Fruits but the Vintage exteriors are all from the Jefferson moulds. Jefferson called this pattern #245 and colors are white, blue, and green with the white occasionally being decorated with a goofus painted treatment.

Vulcan

When I first received the photo of this very attractive spooner, I was quite puzzled about the pattern. Only after a good deal of digging and some mental compromising did I come to the conclusion this is the Vulcan pattern, first made at National Glass in 1900, and then at Ohio Flint Glass of Lancaster, Ohio, in 1902. The crystal items known in this pattern are staggering and include table sets, toothpick holders, salts, 8" compote, celery vase, sauce, syrup, cruet, wine, olive dish, and a vase, but at this point we can only surmise the table set was made in opalescent glass. Reproduced by Fenton.

*Victorian Stripe with
Flowers*

Vintage

Vulcan

127

War of Roses

Waffle

Waterlily and Cattails (Fenton)

War of Roses

A pretty pattern from England's George Davison & Company, War of Roses can be found in either blue or canary opalescent glass (I suspect white was also made) in novelty bowls and the boat-shaped bowl on tiny feet that is shown. The pattern dates from 1885, and is quality in all ways. The design is not really a true rose and more closely resembles a stylized shell, with a row of beading along the bottom.

Waffle

I know very little about the origin of this attractive epergne except it originally came from Germany, carried by hand aboard a commercial airline a few years ago. It stands some 20" tall on an ornate metal base and the lily fits into a metal cup. The beautiful waffle design is olive green, shading to an attractive pink just before the opalescent edging starts. The glass is very fine and thin and is mould blown.

Waterlily and Cattails (Fenton)

The Fenton version of this pattern in opalescent glass is known in several shapes including table sets, water sets, berry sets, a tri-cornered bon-bon, a square bon-bon, a rosebowl, handled relish, bowl novelties, plates, and a breakfast set consisting of an individual creamer and sugar. Colors are white, green, blue, and amethyst as well as carnival glass items.

Waterlily and Cattails (Northwood)

In carnival glass, Northwood made this pattern in only a water set so it isn't surprising to find only the very scarce tumbler showing up in opalescent glass. The example shown is marked with the Northwood mark. Blue is the only color I've heard about and this tumbler in opalescent glass dates to 1905. I'd love to hear from anyone who has seen the matching pitcher or other opalescent colors in this Northwood version.

Waterlily and Cattails (Northwood)

Wheel and Block

Shown as early as 1905 in ads with other Dugan Glass patterns, Wheel and Block has been seen in deep bowls, a vase whimsey and a square plate, all from the same mould. Colors are blue, green, and white with the latter sometimes having a goofus treatment as on the square plate shown.

Wheel and Block

Wide Panel

Here is the second Northwood epergne design, called Wide Panel or Colonial by some collectors. It is well known in carnival glass and is equally respected in opalescent colors of green, white, or blue. Notice that the four lily receiving tubes have been moulded into the glass and the whole design sweeps in a wide paneling from lily to the base. It is less formal than the first epergne design, Thread and Rib, and has no metal in the fittings at all! The fall Butler Brothers catalog of 1909 lists this in opalescent colors at $1.25 each and the 1913 April catalog from the same concern has the carnival glass at $1.50 a piece! How times have changed.

Wide Panel

Wide Stripe

Wild Bouquet

Wild Daffodils

Wide Stripe

I believe this shade was made by the Nickel-Plate Glass Company about 1890. Colors known are cranberry, blue, white and green opalescent. And while both Fenton and Imperial made similar versions of these shades in the late 1930s, the shaping was different. Wide Stripe is known in water sets, cruets, syrups, sugar shakers, toothpick holders, salt shakers, and lamp shades.

Wild Bouquet

Apparently Northwood first made the opalescent pieces in this pattern while a part of National, and the design was then continued by Dugan/Diamond. Shapes made are table sets, berry sets, water sets, a cruet, a toothpick holder, salt shakers, and a cruet set on a tray (the same tray as with Chrysanthemum Sprig). Colors in opalescent glass are white, blue, green, and rarely canary; other treatments are custard and possibly Dugan colored glass in blue and green.

Wild Daffodils

When I first saw this mug pattern, I thought the design was the same as the Wild Rose banana bowl shown elsewhere, but on closer examination, it is obvious the floral design is different. The shape of the mug is like Fenton's Orange Tree mug and I feel it is a Fenton pattern. Colors known are amethyst opalescent, white opalescent with gold trim, and the very strange example shown which looks like a thin custard with the same opalescence and gilding. I believe production of this mug dates from the 1909 – 11 era.

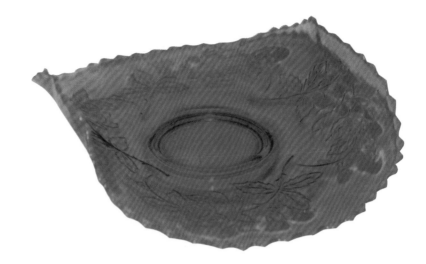

Wild Rose (Fenton's)

Wild Rose (Fenton's)

While I have no proof this interesting pattern is from the Fenton Art Glass Company, I feel safe enough to say I believe it is. First of all, the coloring is a deeper blue that matched known Fenton opalescent production items like Waterlily and Cattails, Honeycomb and Clover, Beaded Stars, and the Hobnail atomizer made for DeVilbiss. In size, the Wild Rose bowl is generous (the banana bowl measures 10½" in length) and the design is simply a raised line drawing just as that found on the Wild Daffodils mug shown above. I haven't tracked any other colors but it was probably made in white opalescent and perhaps green or amethyst.

William and Mary

William and Mary is a Davison Glass product, made in 1903, and found in the usual English opalescent colors of vaseline (canary) and blue. Shapes known are table sets (creamers and open sugars), compotes, a master salt, stemmed cake plate (made from the compote shape), flat plates, and novelty items. The distinctive design elements are the hearts on a line separated by areas of diamond filing.

William and Mary

Wilted Flowers

After additional research, I'm convinced this pattern was made by Dugan/Diamond in Indiana, Pennsylvania, and was part of their Intaglio line. Besides the bowl shapes, there are handled baskets. Some of the white opalescent pieces have a goofus treatment. In addition a Dugan 1909 ad shows the basket with two other Dugan Intaglio products.

Wilted Flowers

131

Windflower

Windflower Nappy

Windows (Plain)

Windflower

Known to be a Dugan Glass Company product that is better known in carnival glass than in opalescent, where it is considered rather rare. First advertised in 1907, the opalescent pieces are known in white and blue and in a 1914 Butler Brothers ad they can be seen along with equally rare opalescent patterns like the Mary Ann vase, the Constellation compote (pulled from the S-Repeat or National goblet shape with an added interior pattern), a Fishscales and Beads bowl, and Stork and Rushes mug and tumbler. A green opalescent Windflower bowl would be a great rarity, but I have no knowledge that one even exists.

Windflower Nappy

Seldom found in carnival glass, this nappy by the Dugan/Diamond company is a real rarity in opalescent glass and to date I've seen only two in white. The bowl in this pattern, shown elsewhere, is part of a very small production run, so to find this nappy is a real surprise. I'd surely like to hear from anyone knowing of additional opalescent colors in this piece if they exist.

Windows (Plain)

Originally a Hobbs, Brockunier pattern, it was later produced by Beaumont Glass and dates to 1889. Shapes known are water sets, finger bowls, bitters bottles, a crimped bowl, oil lamps in several shapes, and two sizes of miniature lamps. Colors known are white, blue, and cranberry. The beautiful pitcher shown has the square top and is a sight to behold.

Windows (Swirled)

Also made by Hobbs, Brockenier, this pattern is sometimes called Hobbs Swirl. The swirl is in the moulding of the glass and can be found in white, blue, and cranberry opalescent. Shapes reported are water sets, cruets, salt shakers, a syrup, table sets, a finger bowl, berry sets, a sugar shaker, a mustard pot, a toothpick holder, and a celery vase. Strangely, the shapes in this pattern all seem to have an oval shape. Production started in 1889.

Windsor Stripe

I feel sure this stripe pattern is English and so I've added the Windsor to establish this. The vase is cranberry with a great amount of opalescence. It stands 4¾" tall, has a six-scallop top and a pontil mark. I would expect other colors and shapes exist and would be happy to hear from anyone about these.

Winter Cabbage

This Dugan pattern very closely resembles another pattern called Cabbage Leaf, also made at Dugan. Both patterns date from 1906, and the difference is the number of leaves, with Winter Cabbage having only three and Cabbage Leaves having overlapping leaves. Winter Cabbage is known in bowls that rest on three vine-like feet that bend back and join the drooping marie of the bowl. Colors are white, green, and blue in opalescent glass.

Windows (Swirled)

Windsor Stripe

Winter Cabbage

Winterlily

Wishbone and Drapery

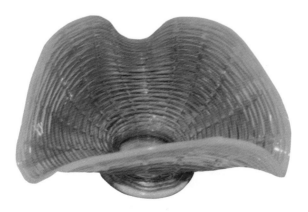

Woven Wonder

Winterlily

Shown in Dugan ads in 1908, this very pretty vase was first made in 1906, in white, blue, and green opalescent glass. It was apparently one of those items made in small amounts for the blue is very hard to find, the green is scarce, and the white seldom found. The mould work is very superior with twig feet turning into rows of vertical beading and a leaf vining around the vase. The lily shape has a glass twist at the top, much like the Cleopatra Fan vase.

Wishbone and Drapery

A Jefferson Glass product from 1903, Wishbone and Drapery is found on bowls and plates in white, green, and blue opalescent. While the design is a pleasant one, it didn't take much imagination and could not be called exciting. However, the coloring is nice, especially on the blue pieces.

Woven Wonder

Made by the Northwood Company, Woven Wonder is actually the same pattern as the exterior of the Rose Show bowl and even the same as Frosted Leaf and Basketweave without the leaf. Perhaps the latter's sugar base was flared for these exterior patterns but I can't prove it. At any rate, Woven Wonder can be found in novelty bowls like the tri-cornered one shown, as well as rose bowls, and I suspect even a vase could be in the realm of possibility. Colors reported are white and blue, but green and canary may well have been made.

Wreath and Shell

*W*reath and Shell

Made in a wide variety of colors and types of glass, Wreath and Shell can be found in white, blue, vaseline, and green opalescent glass, as well as crystal, decorated crystal, and gilded. The pattern was made by the Model Flint Glass Company of Albany, Indiana, around 1900, and can be found in water sets, table sets, berry sets, celery vase, toothpick holder, rose bowl, lady's spittoon, cracker jar, salt dip, and novelties including bowls.

*W*reathed Cherry

While some of these opalescent items in this well-known Dugan/Diamond Glass Company pattern are suspected to be reproductions, this very pretty creamer looks old to me. The glass quality is identical to other Dugan items of the 1909 period and the opalescence is outstanding. There is some wear on the base and the glass weight is more like old. At any rate, you should buy with caution. Shapes reported are table set pieces, but in carnival glass water sets, table sets, oval berry sets, and a very questionable toothpick holder are known. *Never buy this toothpick holder in opalescent glass, for all are new!*

*Z*ipper and Loops

This large vase was a Jefferson Glass Company product, dating from 1908. It can be found in the usual opalescent glass colors of green, white, and blue. While attractive, it certainly isn't a showstopper, but it does fit very nicely in a collection of vases and is of a useable size being some 11½" tall.

Wreathed Cherry

Zipper and Loops

Part II: *Whimsey Pieces*

Webster's Dictionary defines a whimsey as an odd fancy and that definition certainly fits the glass items in this section.

Generally speaking, the glassmakers were very skilled artisans and liked nothing better than to show off these skills. Often, when they grew bored or tired of the same shapes being turned out, they produced one of these odd fancies that was not a part of regular production but could nevertheless be sold as either a novelty or sometimes given to a friend or loved one as a special gift. Many whimsies were made to be slipped out of the factory by the glassmaker at the end of the day, to be taken home and presented to a wife or family member.

For these reasons, whimsies have become a very loved part of glass collecting and it is a pleasure to show a few examples here so that the collector of today may understand just what whimsies are and how attractive they may be.

And perhaps I should also say that some whimsies were so popular they did go into limited production from pattern to following pattern. Such examples of lady's spittoons as I show here became very popular and were produced over the years on many types of glass, especially in the years of carnival glass production, until they were no longer considered whimsies at all!

Many whimsies, however, are a bit grotesque in their shaping and seem strange indeed to us today. Just remember, every one of these odd fancies was the product of a master craftsman in the days when glassmaking was an art. Enjoy them!

Argonaut Shell (Nautilus) Tray

Argonaut Shell (Nautilus) Tray

This whimsey item was originally the sugar base in the table set before it was stretched and turned into this very attractive whimsey card tray. As you can see, the color is vaseline but it can be found in white and blue as well. This piece is one of those whimsies that were apparently quite popular for they were made in some number.

Astro Hat

This hat whimsey, made from the common bowl shape, is actually much prettier than the original shape, and could have even been pulled into a vase! It just shows what a little imagination and a good bit of skill can do in adding to the design.

Autumn Leaves Whimsey

It's a real privilege to show this banana bowl whimsey in Autumn Leaves because it is the rare green opalescent glass. For years this pattern was reported in white and blue only, but as you can see, green exists and would be a real find for any collection.

Astro Hat

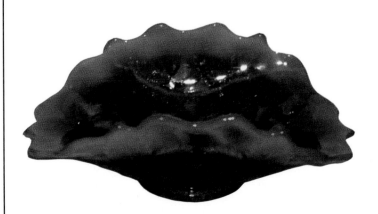

Autumn Leaves Whimsey

Blooms and Blossoms Proof
Nappy

Blown Twist Celery Whimsey

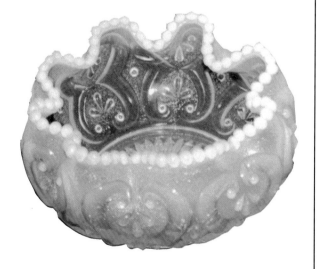

Cashews Rose Bowl

Blooms and Blossoms Proof Nappy

Occasionally, you will find a piece of old glass that has only part of the design finished. These are called "proofs" and are very collectible. On the nappy shown here the outline of the blossoms and the leaves are there but the detail of the design is missing! Since only a few of these pieces were produced before the finished design was completed, these proof pieces are always scarcer than the normal pattern.

Blown Twist Celery Whimsey

While this isn't truly a whimsey in the strict sense of the word, this is the first celery vase *ever* reported in this rare pattern and as you can see the top is edged with a cranberry decoration! Seen in white, blue, or vaseline opalescent.

Cashews Rose Bowl

Apparently the Northwood Company permitted artistic license in workers, for many whimsey shapes came from this company. Here is the pretty Cashews pattern, normally found on bowls or plates, but pulled up and ruffled into a stunning rose bowl. When I first saw this piece I fell in love with it.

Cashews Whimsey Bowl

Cashews Whimsey Bowl

It is hard to imagine a bowl more whimsied than this one shown. The rim is pulled into three extreme peaks and the rest is rolled into a low flowing sweep that gives the piece an almost unusable shape. It does have a strange appeal however and certainly would be a conversation piece.

Daisy and Fern

While the piece shown isn't a true whimsey, it is seen so seldom in any type of glass, I wanted to show it here. It is the Daisy and Fern pattern in a shape known as a finger bowl. I doubt it was ever used as such and must have had a different purpose but I have no idea what. It measures 4½" across and 3" high.

Daisy and Fern

Daisy and Plume

What makes this footed bowl a whimsey is not only the depth of the bowl but the very odd way the top is ruffled into square shapes. I can't recall another pattern with this exact same crimping, either from Northwood or Dugan.

Daisy and Plume

Fan Card Tray

Feathers Bowl

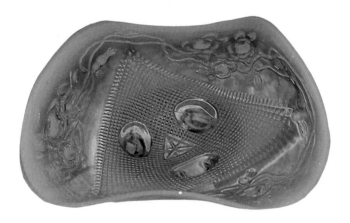

Finecut and Roses Whimsey Bowl

*F*an Card Tray

A bit flatter than the Argonaut Shell card tray whimsey shown earlier, this piece shows the Dugan/Diamond Glass workers were just as skilled. This piece was made from the spooner in the table set. Two of the edges have been extended to elongate the piece and add interest. Oddly enough, this pattern was also whimsied into a gravy boat with handle that is often found in carnival glass.

*F*eathers Bowl

Here is a real rarity! Pulled from the well-known Northwood vase pattern, this is the *only* example of the whimsey bowl shape I've ever seen or heard about. It certainly is an outstanding item. Surely more were made but where are they? The vase can be found in blue and green also, so keep your eyes open. This piece has a base diameter of 3⅝", is 2½" high, with a bowl diameter of 8½".

*F*inecut and Roses Whimsey Bowl

It is hard to imagine this piece of glass was whimsied from the same mould as the footed bowl shown in Part I but it has simply been flattened out and the edges rolled up on four sides. Actually this was a pretty standard practice on this pattern in opalescent glass. I've seen several of these pieces in blue, white, and green.

*F*lora Banana Bowl

Flora is a Beaumont Glass pattern and the whimsey shown was made from the butter dish base. The top has been pulled to make it oval and then heavily ruffled giving it a very pretty look. I've heard there is one of these with an applied handle spanning the center but haven't seen it. The same shape with a handle does appear in many later items, especially from the Dugan/Diamond Company in carnival glass.

*F*luted Bars and Beads Whimsey Rose Bowl

A look at this piece will reveal it is simply the compote shape that has been pulled in at the top into a rose bowl shape. As I've said earlier, this pattern has been credited to the Northwood Company but I really believe it was a Jefferson Glass pattern. Colors known in the whimsey shape are white, blue, green, and vaseline.

*F*rosted Leaf and Basketweave Whimsey Vase

This vase, whimsied from the spoon holder, stands 7½" tall and in my opinion is more attractive than the spooner itself in design. Made by Northwood in 1905, all other known pieces are from the table set also and I feel the vase whimsey shape must be the rarest of all shapes. Colors are blue and white opalescent so far, but certainly the vaseline was made. These vases range from 7" to 12".

Flora Banana Bowl

*Fluted Bars and Beads
Whimsey Rose Bowl*

*Frosted Leaf and
BaketweaveWhimsey
Vase*

141

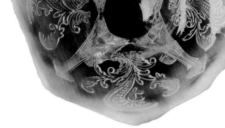

Inverted Fan and Feather Card Tray

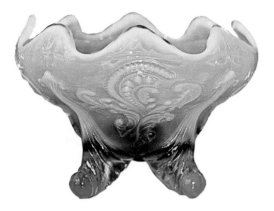

*Inverted Fan and Feather
Large Whimsey Rose Bowl*

*Inverted Fan and Feather
Spittoon*

*I*nverted Fan and Feather Card Tray

I fell in love with this cutie the first time I saw it and am not ashamed to say so. It was whimsied from the spooner and is a real find. I've seen blue and vaseline but white surely is known.

*I*nverted Fan and Feather Large Whimsey Rose Bowl

Here is a rose bowl whimsey shaped from the large berry bowl and as such is a true delight. It was made by Dugan/Diamond and probably in the usual colors of white, blue, canary, and green which is a scarce color in this pattern. The piece shown measures 4" tall and 5½" across the top.

*I*nverted Fan and Feather Spittoon

Here is one of the very attractive spittoon whimsey pieces pulled from the spooner shape. In carnival glass, these pieces are called lady's spittoons, for rumor has it that women actually were the users! I can't verify this, but my great-grandmother did smoke a clay pipe so maybe they were tobacco chewers, too.

Inverted Fan and
Feather Rose Bowl

*I*nverted Fan and Feather Rose Bowl

Also from the spooner shape, this whimsey item was so popular it was actually produced in greater amounts and eventually even advertised by the Northwood Company. It was long felt by some collectors to be a new item but that proved to be untrue since this whimsey piece was advertised in a 1901 National ad after Northwood's admission into the combine.

*I*nverted Fan and Feather Vase

Shown in a 1908 Butler Brothers ad of Dugan/Diamond items, this very scarce vase was a carryover at the factory and was made in limited amounts in blue, green, and white opalescent glass. It is the first I've been privileged to see.

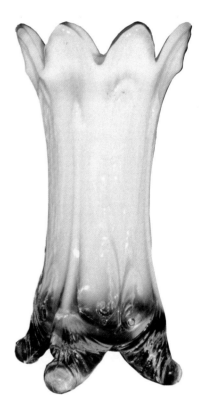

Inverted Fan and
Feather Vase

*J*ewel and Fan Whimsey

Known in two sizes, this Jefferson pattern has been whimsied into a banana bowl shape. Actually it is quite nice and shows the pattern well. As I said earlier, the design is simple but very effective.

Jewel and Fan Whimsey

143

Jewels and Drapery Bowl

Keyhole Bowl

Lattice Medallions

Jewels and Drapery Bowl

Here is the whimsey bowl shape that was flattened from the vase shape shown elsewhere. While the vase is a difficult item to find, the whimsey is just plain rare!

Keyhole Bowl

Here is an example of a whimsey that is like the original shape. The only thing that qualifies this piece as a whimsey is the tri-cornered shape of the top and the dipping of one side of the triangle like a jack-in-the-pulpit shape. This configuration was quite popular and all companies made some bowls in similar shapes, especially in the carnival glass era. Keyhole is a Dugan/Diamond item and was made in goofus, carnival, and opalescent glass.

Lattice Medallions

What a pretty whimsey this nut bowl shape is. And while Northwood was not known for items whimsied into this shape, a few examples are known, especially in carnival glass. Please note the unusual knobby feet on this pattern. They seem to go unnoticed with the usual bowl shape but show to advantage here.

Leaf and Beads Bowl

Leaf and Beads Bowl

Generally found in a rose bowl or candy bowl shape, this piece has been stretched into a rough triangle and then had the three corners reshaped to give it a very odd look. One corner has been pulled down, the other two are almost level and the back area opposite the dropped corner is raised!

Leaf and Beads (Flame)

Shaped much like the other whimsey shown in this pattern, this example has the flames on the edging pulled to very exaggerated points, making this an attractive and unusual piece.

Leaf Chalice Rose Bowl Whimsey

Here's the Northwood Leaf Chalice in one of its many whimsey shapes and this one is my favorite. All four leaves are pulled up and tucked in to form a very pretty design. This shape shows the design to the fullest without any distortion. It has been seen in all colors.

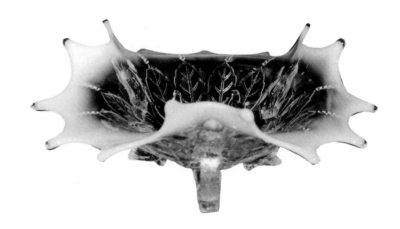

Leaf and Beads (Flame)

Leaf Chalice Rose Bowl

145

Many Loops Rose Bowl Whimsey

Many Loops Tri-Cornered Bowl

Ocean Shell

Many Loops Rose Bowl Whimsey

While this isn't one of my favorite patterns from the Jefferson Company, I do like this rose bowl whimsey shape and could certainly find room for one in my collection. I know of these in blue and green, so I'm sure the white was made also. Of course, many collectors look for rose bowls and this is a good one.

Many Loops Tri-Cornered Bowl

The tri-cornered effect on this Jefferson bowl is quite easy to see and typifies the crimping that gives this very nice shaping. Please remember the tri-cornered bowls generally sell for about 20 percent more than round ones, so its a point to look for.

Ocean Shell

Not as obvious as some whimsey pieces, this Ocean Shell relies on the one edge being pulled out to form a tail-like section while the opposite side has been scooped into a small spout. It is almost as if the glassmaker wanted to form a gravy boat without the handle!

Open O's Rose Bowl Whimsey

Open O's Rose Bowl Whimsey

What a pleasant surprise this pretty rose bowl was when I first saw it. I debated whether to call it a rose bowl whimsey or a spittoon whimsey but since the top is turned in it must be a rose bowl. It is Northwood of course, and may well have been made in other colors like the other shapes.

Palm and Scroll Rose Bowl Whimsey

Again, here is a whimsey shape that is much nicer that the original bowl shape. Dugan/Diamond is the maker and they certainly made the right move when they made this piece. The feather-like palms seem to be made just for this shape. Colors are blue, white, and green.

Piasa Bird Spittoon

Probably no other pattern in opalescent glass can be found in more whimsey shapes than this one. This one is the spittoon shape and while it became an in-line item, it is nevertheless a whimsey shape as are all spittoons. All Piasa Bird whimsey pieces were shaped from the bowl shape.

Palm and Scroll Rose Bowl Whimsey

Piasa Bird Spittoon

147

Piasa Bird Vase

Piasa Bird Rose Bowl

Reflecting Diamonds

*P*iasa Bird Vase

Much like the regular vase in this pattern, this whimsey has one top flame pulled into a grotesque spike and it is for this reason it has to be called a whimsey. Just what the glassmaker had in mind is hard to imagine. Surely he didn't just have a bad day, for several of these vase whimsey pieces are known.

*P*iasa Bird Rose Bowl

Here is the third whimsey in this pattern and it really shows the design as well as any piece I've seen. For some reason, blue seems to the be the color most found in these pieces and I've seen more rose bowls than spittoons. Oddly, some collectors know this pattern by other names (Old Man of the Sea or Demonic) but Piasa seems to be the name most used.

*R*eflecting Diamonds

The ice cream bowl isn't an ordinary shape for this Dugan pattern and in fact, few bowls from this company are found in this shape. For novices, ice cream bowls are round without ruffling and have a slightly turned in edge.

*Reverse
Drapery
Whimsey
Vase*

Reverse Drapery Whimsey Vase

If you will look closely at the Boggy Bayou vase shown in the first section as well as the bowl in Reverse Drapery, you will see just how this whimsey vase, from the bowl, has been widely confused with the Boggy Bayou vase. The design on the marie is quite different however and starts higher above the marie. In addition, the top flaming is very different and usually has little flare.

Roulette Square Plate

Just as tri-cornered bowls are very collectible, so are squared plates and bowls. Here, the standard Roulette bowl has been first flattened to a plate and then the four opposing corners pulled to a square, making a very pleasing design.

Ruffles and Rings Nut Bowl

I apologize for mislabeling this pattern as Wreath and Shell in the first edition of this book but I plead eye-strain from viewing so many photos at the time. This scarce nut bowl was shaped from the regular bowl shape amd may well have been made in other colors besides the blue shown and the white example I've since seen. It is a scarce whimsey and very collectible in any color.

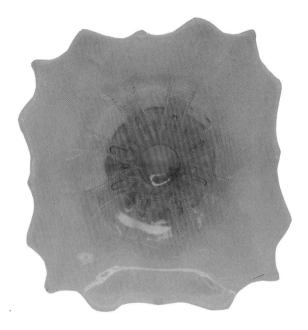

Roulette Square Plate

Ruffles and Rings Nut Bowl

Sea Spray Whimsey Nappy

Shell and Dots Nut Bowl Whimsey

Singing Bird Whimsey

Sea Spray Whimsey Nappy

Made from the same mould as the round example shown earlier, this tri-cornered piece has an appeal all its own. The edges have been pulled to form a triangle shape. Colors seen in this configuration are blue, white, and green — just like the round ones.

Shell and Dots Nut Bowl Whimsey

Earlier I showed this pattern in a rose-bowl and that is usually how it is seen. There are variations, however, and here is one of them. Here the bowl has been pulled into a deep, square shape with only a small flare of the outer rim giving it the appearance we call a nutbowl shape. Shell and Dots can also be found in regular bowl shapes, but oddly, these are fewer than the other shapes.

Singing Bird Whimsey

Previously unreported, this very rare whimsey, pulled from a tumbler into a hat shape, is the only known example in opalescent glass. The color matches the opalescent mug in this pattern and the glass is clear and sparkling. Is it possible a water set exists in opalescent treatment or even a carnival glass tumbler in aqua opalescent, since this rare carnival color is made with blue opalescent pieces? I'd be very happy to hear from anyone who has more information on this whimsey.

Squirrel and Acorn Vase

If you will compare this with the standard compote in this pattern shown earlier you will see just how much of a whimsey this piece has become, especially with the three flattened flames that are almost comical. But despite this odd shaping, this piece is quite attractive and would add much to any collection, especially since the pattern is so very rare.

Stripe Rose Bowl

While in the strictest sense of the word, this shape isn't a true whimsey, the example shown is likely British and indeed the shape seems to be a whimsey in this production. As you can see there is no collar base and there is a pontil break mark on the base. The coloring is quite good and I suspect this piece can be found in white and canary, as well as, the blue shown.

Stripe Spittoon Whimsey

This beautiful piece of glass is 3" tall, 4" wide, and has a top opening of less than 1". It is blown glass and may well be of English origin although the shape seems to indicate it isn't. Many American companies made a Stripe product and it could be from any of these, especially Northwood, but I can't be sure. Any information on this piece would be greatly appreciated.

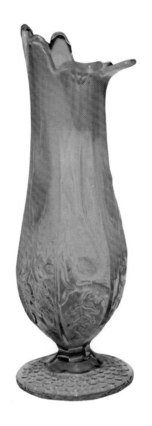

Squirrel and Acorn Vase

Stripe Rose Bowl

Stripe Spittoon Whimsey

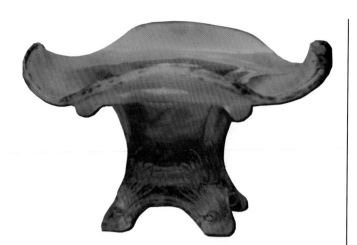

Swag with Brackets Sugar Base

Swirl Spittoon Whimsey

*Thread and Rib Whimsey
Epergne*

S *wag with Brackets Sugar Base*

Just why Jefferson made these whimsey pieces from the sugar base is a mystery to me! And then to top them with the cranberry fritt edging seems to be a bit much; nevertheless, I've seen these in all the opalescent colors Jefferson made and most had the cranberry decoration (a few even had gilding on the legs). I suppose they could be used as nut or mint dishes!

S *wirl Spittoon Whimsey*

It is difficult to say just who made this particular whimsey since just about all glassmakers had a try at this design. If I had to guess, I'd be inclined to say Northwood, but don't hold me to that. At any rate it is a super piece of glass and worth owning.

T *hread and Rib Whimsey Epergne*

The reason I call this piece a whimsey is that the edges of the base are pulled into flames and then fanned in waves. Please compare this piece with the pattern shown elsewhere and you will readily see the difference.

Twigs J.I.P. Whimsey

Twigs J.I.P. Whimsey

Here is still another whimsey shape in this nice vase pattern, and next to the pulled wing example shown elsewhere, it is the most desirable. Coloring is right and the opalescence is outstanding.

Twigs Vase

This Dugan vase is one of the prettiest whimsies made and for this reason was produced in some amounts although not nearly so many as to be production shaping for more than a few months. As you can see, the top has been opened and pulled into four wing-like ruffles that really give life and character to this vase and make it much more attractive than the regular shapings shown elsewhere in this book.

Twister Vase Whimsey

Perhaps this vase isn't a true whimsey and there may well be more of these out there, but the Twister pattern is known as a bowl or plate pattern and this is the first vase I've heard about. The design has been pulled straight up rather than in a twist like the bowl items so while it doesn't look the same, the marie is the same and the line configurations are identical. Jefferson made the Twister pattern.

Twigs Vase

Twister Vase Whimsey

153

Waterlily and Cattail Rose Bowl Whimsey

Waterlily and Cattail Rose Bowl Whimsey

Here's another one of the well-known patterns, this time by Fenton, turned into a pretty rose bowl whimsey. The color is a strong amethyst opalescent, one color that only Fenton seems to have made. I've seen these in both white and blue opalescent glass also, but the amethyst would be the choice color to own.

Wreath and Shell Bowl Whimsey

Flared and ruffled, this whimsey bowl measures 6½" across the top and stands a bit over 3" tall. One often hears these pieces described as novelty bowls but to be precise, when they are made from another shape, they are truly whimsies. It was probably made in all opalescent colors.

Wreath and Shell Spittoon

Made by the Model Flint Glass Company of Albany, Indiana, this pattern had several whimsey versions, all from the table set spooner and I am showing three of these. Here is the spittoon and there seems to be several examples of this shape in blue, white, and canary. All are quite collectible and sought after by advanced buyers.

Wreath and Shell Bowl Whimsey

Wreath and Shell Spittoon

Wreath and Shell Rose Bowl

*W*reath and Shell
   Rose Bowl

Just like the spittoon whimsey previously shown, this piece came from the spooner shape and had the lips turned in to make a rose bowl. I think this shape is much prettier than the spittoon whimsey, but fewer of these seem to be around. Maybe they just didn't survive as well. At any rate, they are very collectible and highly prized.

*W*reath and Shell
   Whimsey Ivy Ball

Shaped from the flat tumbler (tumblers in this pattern can be flat based, or footed), this whimsey is called an ivy ball and it is one of my very favorite pieces in this pattern. It is rare and very collectible, and I wish I owned one!

Wreath and Shell Whimsey Ivy Ball

Part III: *Opalescent Glass After 1930*

Wherever I've gone to photograph items for this book, I've found examples of glass made after the time frame generally accepted as old opalescent glass. Some of this newer glass is very attractive in its own right and some is an obvious attempt to copy old patterns.

For the sake of identification I've decided to show a sampling of these items so that the collector will be aware of them but I purposely *do not price these new items* since I catalog *only old glass.*

Actually an entire book could be filled with new items and many more are being produced every year; with the examples here we are only breaking the surface. When collecting, be alert, handle as much glass and you can, study it (both old and new). You will soon be able to tell a difference and in most cases will not find yourself paying huge prices for new glass or reproductions.

Remember, the majority of the patterns (approximately 90 percent) *have not been reproduced!* Of course, I do not have to tell you that patterns like Hobnail, Coinspot, Swirl, and Stripe have many copies and should only be purchased as old once you are comfortable with your knowledge. Buy only from a reputable dealer who will stand behind the sale if you do suspect your purchase to be questionable.

Beyond that, all I can say is "Happy Hunting!"

Acorn and Leaf Chalice

*A*corn and Leaf Chalice

Here is a brand new item I've received several inquiries about. It is a shame some flea markets and mall dealers are selling these at old glass prices! This new chalice has been seen in white, emerald green, and vaseline opalescent glass, and has been distributed by a company that sells only new items, usually by a mail listing. Other repo items such as opalescent Dugan Dahlia pieces and Beaded Shell pieces are listed in their catalog so beware!

*A*tomizers

In the late 1920s and early 1930s the Fenton Company made beautiful glass atomizers for the DeVilbiss Company, who were marketers and producers of the metal atomizer parts. Since the DeVilbiss products have become quite collectible, these beautifully made glass ones are now sought by many collectors. Shown are three examples: Hobnail (1928), Cosmos FLower (1932), and Petticoats (1933).

Hobnail Atomizer

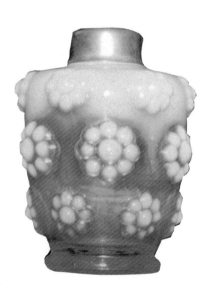

Cosmos Flower Atomizer

Petticoats Atomizer

Coin Dot (Fenton)

Corn Vase Reproduction

C oin Dot (Fenton)

Here are two Fenton items in cranberry Coin Dot Spot. The vase was their #194 and was made first in 1948, while the barber bottle, which stands 8½" tall, was made in the 1950s. Both pieces, despite being recent glass, are quality all the way as Fenton products are.

C orn Vase Reproduction

If you compare this new vase with the originals shown earlier, you can readily see the top isn't pulled like the old ones and in addition, the husks are solid glass from outer edge to the vase itself, not open like those Dugan/Diamond originally made. The repos have been seen in blue, vaseline, and a strange pale blue that had no opalescence. These repos are credited to L.G. Wright from the 1950s to the 1960s, so be sure of what you have before you buy.

Daisy and Button

Daisy and Button

Here is a rather scarce item from the Fenton Company. It was made in 1938 in both blue and white opalescent glass, but seldom enters discussions or is found for sale. Fenton has, over the years, made numerous items in this pattern. This bon-bon is listed as their #1900. The blue is rather light in color.

Daisy and Fern

Made for L. G. Wright by Fenton in the 1940s, this canary opalescent barber bottle with a satin finish is attractive enough, but the collector should know Daisy and Fern pattern was not made in this color in old glass.

Daisy and Fern

Fenton Daisy and Fern

*Daisy and Fern Cruet
(Fenton)*

Daisy and Fern (Fenton)
This very attractive pitcher is shown in the 1983 L.G. Wright catalogs and was produced by Fenton for them. As you can see, the handle is reeded, a warning sign. Colors are cranberry, cobalt blue, and this beautiful vaseline. Now as far as buying such a nice piece, there certainly is a place for such quality in collecting as long as you know it is new and as long as you pay new prices for it.

Daisy and Fern Cruet (Fenton)
Like the other pieces reproduced by the Fenton Company for L. G. Wright in 1983, this pretty cruet has a reeded handle. It was made in cranberry, blue, cobalt, and vaseline. Other shapes made were sugar shakers, barber bottles, and syrups, so be careful when you buy. In addition the catalogs show a sugar and creamer set as well as a tall creamer that looks like a miniature pitcher.

Diamond Optic Perfume Bottle

Here is another Fenton pattern, made in the 1980s, in white, blue, and cranberry. The globe-like stopper is commonly seen on new pieces so be very cautious in buying perfumes. Most are new, except for a few European pieces.

Duncan and Miller

This well-known firm was organized in 1874, and over the years has made many types of glass. It is their opalescent items, made in the 1920s and 1930s that most impress collectors today. For this reason I'm showing two examples of their work. First, an ashtray in vaseline opalescent glass from a line known as Sanibel. It has a very modern look, came in many colors, and certainly would not be confused with old glass. Next is a pale blue opalescent vase called "Cogs et Plume." Its artistic quality is obvious and compares with items from Lalique glass.

Eye Dot

Another repo from L. G. Wright, this beautiful oil lamp is a quality item and would be an asset to any collector. Just don't pay old prices for it and you'll be fine.

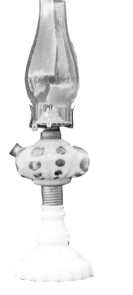

Eye Dot

Duncan and Miller Vase

Duncan and Miller Ashtray

*Diamond Optic
Perfume Bottle*

161

Fenton Coindot Basket

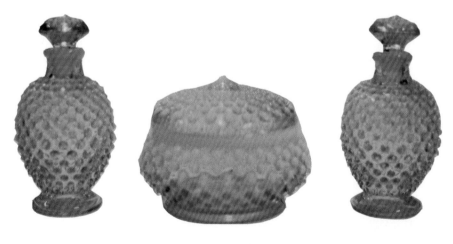

Fenton Hobnail

*F*enton Coindot Basket

First made about 1947, this basket shape has a lot of quality, as do nearly all Fenton products, but the giveaway as to age is two-fold. First is the shape, not found in old opalescent American glass and most prominent, the sectioned handled that so looks like bamboo. Remember, unless you are confident about age, always avoid reeded or sectioned handles!

*F*enton Hobnail

The fan vase shown was first produced in opalescent glass in 1940, and was a part of a very extensive line that included a water set, table set, vases, bowls, hats, slippers, covered compotes, baskets, syrup jugs, a dresser tray, a rose bowl, shakers, goblets, a plate, and even an epergne. Colors were blue, white, green, vaseline, and cranberry. Various parts of this line continued for more than a decade in production.

Fenton Hobnail Water Set

*F*enton Hobnail Water Set

While there are many, many shapes in this Fenton line, made for many years (this set dates to 1952), this very nice water set is too attractive not to show. The pitcher is squat and has a reeded handle and heavy collar base as do the tumblers. This set, as well as other Fenton Hobnail pieces of the period were made in all sorts of glass and many colors as well.

*F*enton's Heart Opal

Here is another perfume (minus the stopper) the Fenton Company made from 1978 to 1985 in both white and cranberry opalescent glass. Other shapes I've seen are creamers and handled baskets, but certainly many others are possible. This design is pretty enough to collect, but avoid paying old prices for glass this recent.

Fenton's Heart Opal

Fenton's Hobnail Fan Vase

Fenton's Hobnail Candy Compote

Fenton's Hobnail Fan Vase

The fan vase shown was first produced in opalescent glass in 1940, and was a part of a very extensive line that included a water set, table set, vases, bowls, hats, slippers, covered compotes, baskets, syrup jugs, a dresser tray, a rose bowl, shakers, goblets, a plate, and even an epergne. Colors were blue, white, green, vaseline, and cranberry. Various parts of this line continued in production for more than a decade.

Fenton's Hobnail Candy Compote

While this is a very pretty item that dates to 1959, it certainly isn't old opalescent glass. Made for several years, colors are topaz (vaseline), green, blue, plum (purple), and cranberry. Numbered 3887, Fenton's Hobnail was made in many types of glass and in many shapes including covered bowls, open bowls, compotes (several sizes), candlesticks, vases, slippers, fairy lamps, bon-bons, planters, creamers and ash trays, wines, decanters, handled baskets, and epergnes.

Fenton's Hobnail Lamps

Shown are two very different lamps with blue opalescent hobnail founts that were made by the Fenton Glass Company in the early 1930s. These founts were supplied to several lamp makers who then turned out these very attractive lamps. Colors reported are blue, white, and cranberry.

Fenton Spanish Lace

This very pretty Fenton reproduction is so very well done, it compares favorably with old pieces, but aside from being marked, this piece has a reeded handle that has to be a warning! Just remember, the Fenton Company has made many patterns and pieces over the years in opalescent glass and most have been well cataloged in three Fenton books, so there is little reason to mistake these pieces. Add to that the fact that Fenton began marking all their glass in 1970, and the task becomes simple.

Fenton's Hobnail Lamps

Fenton Spanish Lace

Fenton Swirl Bowl

Fenton Swirl Bowl

Shown is a very attractive Swirl bowl made by the Fenton Glass Company in 1939. It sits atop one of their standards that were sold as both bowl stands and a base for the hurricane shades made at the time. These bases can by found in royal blue and milk glass.

Fenton Swirl Vase

The Fenton Company started making this vase in the 1930s, and it has been popular over the years. The company called this vase pattern Spiral. Other shapes are known, such as candlesticks, a console bowl, a 10½" triangle vase, and a large hat vase. The vase shown is 8" tall. Colors are varied including French opalescent, blue, green, cranberry, and possibly others. Some pieces have a contrasting cased edge.

Floral Eyelet (Daisy Eye Dot)

Also made for the L.G. Wright Company by Fenton, this very nice copy is called Daisy Eye Dot in their advertising in 1982. The original pattern was the very rare Floral Eyelet, of course. Again the giveaways are the reeded handle and the shape of the pitcher (old Floral Eyelet pitchers are *not* cannonball shaped). However, there again is a new item well worth owning if you do not buy it as old and pay a new price for it.

Fenton Swirl Vase

Floral Eyelet (Daisy Eye Dot)

166

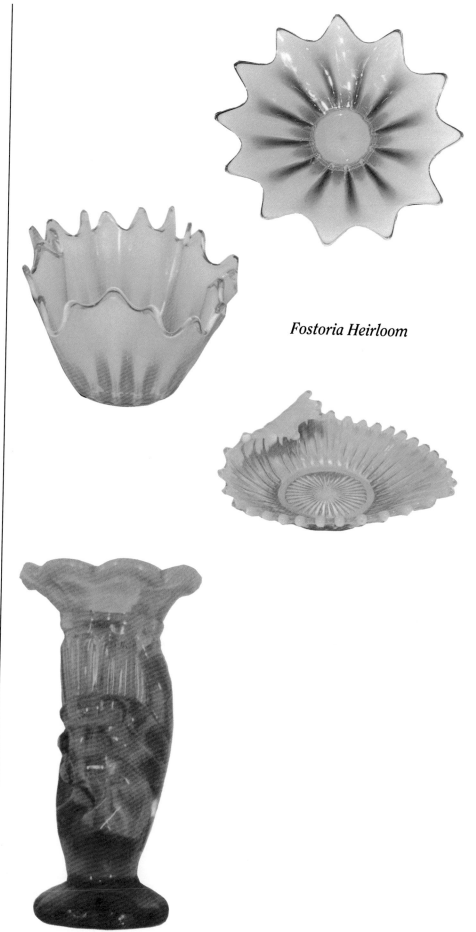

Fostoria Heirloom

Here are three shapes that were all grouped in Fostoria's Heirloom line, made between 1959 and 1970. The bowl was listed as #2183, the star-shaped plate as #2570, and the rolled novelty bowl that I called Rolled Rib as #2727. This latter piece had several shapes including a deep bowl and the other two items were also available in more shapes. I've seen these items in green, white, cranberry (light), and two shades of blue, the one shown and a very light airy one. The quality of all these items is outstanding and should be collected with the best of glass items dating to the 1960s and 1970s.

Hand Vase

Despite being a newer item, made by Fenton in 1942 as their #38, I find this 4" cutie very attractive. It has the quality Fenton is known for and fairly good opalescence.

Fostoria Heirloom

Hand Vase

Hobnail Puff Box

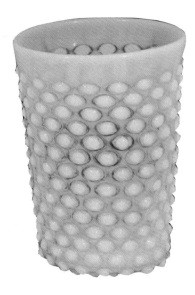

Hobnail Tumbler

Hobnail Variant

Hobnail (Czechoslovakian)

Made in the 1950s, these two pieces, a cranberry puff box with cover and a vaseline tumbler, are very pretty examples of the world famous Hobnail pattern, this time made in Czechoslovakia. Note that the hobs go all the way over the bottom of these pieces. I've seen several items including small dishes, a small vase, and perfume bottles that match the puff box. Colors I know about are cranberry, vaseline, a very dark blue, and a dark green.

Hobnail Variant

I've called this Hobnail pattern a variant because of the odd seam-like sections that are on opposite sides of the piece. I've named this a "zipper mould" because it looks just like a zipper's fittings to me. It was made in the late 1940s and early 1950s in several shapes. Quality-wise, it isn't top-notch.

Keystone Colonial (Fenton)

While this handled compote looks just like the well-known Keystone Colonial made by Westmoreland decades earlier, this is a new piece made by the Fenton Company in the 1990s. It is marked with the familiar F in a circle with the #9, indicating the decade in the 1900s, a very helpful marking practice I wish all modern glass makers would use. The coloring and opalescence are very good.

Keystone Colonial (Fenton)

Lace Edged Buttons

Lace Edged Buttons

This Imperial pattern dates from 1937, and was still being made in 1942. I've seen more than one shape but all had the open-edged treatment. Colors are blue, green, or white, but there may well be others. While attractive, the value isn't much more than it was when these items were made.

Lace Edged Diamonds

Like its close companion, Lace Edged Buttons, this is another Imperial pattern made in the late 1930s and early 1940s. As you can see, this pattern has handles. It is a very nice design, made in white, green, and blue, but again, the value is small and only slightly more than when manufactured.

Lace Edged Diamonds

Needlepoint

This is a Fostoria pattern and is signed on the bottom in script. These tumblers were made in three sizes and at least three colors including green (shown), blue, and orange. They first appear in Fostoria ads in 1951, and have no other shapes listed.

Needlepoint

Open-Edge Basketweave

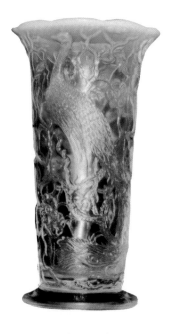

Peacock Garden Vase

Plymouth

Open-Edge Basketweave

While Fenton made this very pattern in old opalescent glass in 1911 – 13, it wasn't made in this royal blue color until 1932, so we can be sure this is a newer piece. Old colors are blue (regular), green, and white, as well as a pastel vaseline.

Peacock Garden Vase

This very beautiful 10" vase in French opalescent glass was a product of the Fenton Company (their #791) and was made in 4", 6", 8", and 10" sizes in 1934. The moulds came from the old Northwood Company, it is believed, where a carnival version was made. Since the early 1930s, Fenton has made this vase (in the 8" size mostly) in over two dozen treatments including a topaz opalescent example in 1988. The 10" example shown is considered quite rare and is very collectible.

Plymouth

In 1935 Fenton made a large line of this pattern, all very useful items including plates, wines, highballs, old fashioned glasses, a rare mug, and this pilsner shown. These were all done in their French opalescent glass and have quality all the way. Additional shapes were added including a cocktail glass and a goblet.

Queen's Petticoat

Only after the first edition of this book came out did I learn this pretty little vase was made by Fostoria in 1959, as part of their Heirloom collection. It was listed as their #5056 and can be found in opalescent colors of yellow, blue, pink, green, ruby, and bittersweet (orange). I am sorry that I may have misled some collectors into thinking this was an old piece but it is just that good!

Ring

Made in 1933 by the Fenton Company, the Ring pitcher is actually very scarce and highly collectible. It stands 7" tall. I'm sure Fenton made this in their usual colors of the time, so green, blue, and vaseline are possibilities.

Spiral Optic (Fenton)

Made in 1939, this pattern was called Spiral Optic by Fenton and could be found in white, blue, and cranberry opalescent. The unusual shape has been called their Barcelona mould by one author, and that may well be just what it is, despite my finding no reference to this in the ads showing this pattern in vases, hat shapes, and other pieces from the same mould.

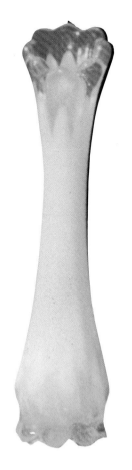

Queen's Petticoat

Ring

Spiral Optic (Fenton)

Spiral Optic Hat

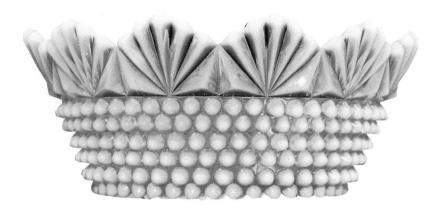

Stamm House Dewdrop

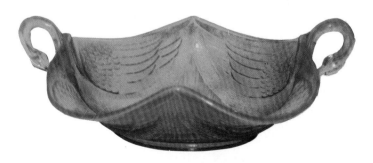

Swan Bowl

Spiral Optic Hat

While Fenton first made their Spiral Optic pattern in 1939, the hat shape shown came along a bit later. The blue opalescent one shown was made in 1952 and again in the 1970s. These hat shapes, as well as vases and baskets from the same mould, were made in several sizes and colors including blue, green, cranberry, and French (white) opalescent. The example shown is 3" tall and measures 3¼" across the top.

Stamm House Dewdrop (#1886/642)

I'm told this pretty 10" bowl was made by Imperial Glass in 1966. Apparently it had saucers to go with it and there may be other shapes also. The coloring (canary) is vivid and beautiful, and anyone not knowing its origin would suspect it to be English. Imperial made little opalescent glass and even though it is relatively new, this piece is certainly collectible.

Swan Bowl

Apparently this bowl and its companion pieces (smaller bowls and candlesticks) were first made at the Dugan/Diamond plant in 1926 – 27, and later at the Fenton Art Glass factory in 1934 – 39. The Dugan/Diamond version is known in pink, green, and black glass and the Fenton pieces are advertised in opalescent colors so it appears the master bowl shown is a Fenton item despite its color matching so many of Dugan's opalescent items in blue. At any rate, these blue pieces are considered rare as are the green opalescent items. Other treatments at the Fenton factory are satinized crystal (1939), amber (1938), amethyst (same year), and the large bowl is currently being made in a pretty misty green.

Tokyo

*T*okyo

If you look closely at the compote shown you can see the color is light, the opalescence thin. The original pattern was made by Jefferson glass in 1905, but this piece when held and examined is obviously not of that quality. I do not know of other shapes having been reproduced but it is possible.

*T*rout

When I first showed this pretty bowl, I had no information about it but speculated it might be French. It is, in fact, Verlys, made by the Holophane Company of France in 1931, so we've moved it from the old glass section. Fenton bought the mould in 1966 and has reproduced this piece. New treatments include an acid finish with opalescence. The bowl has an 8½" diameter and stands 3½" tall.

Trout

*T*wigs (Reproduction)

If you take a close look at the old vase in this pattern shown earlier and this piece you will see several differences. On this reproduction, the twig legs are not open from the vase but have a solid glass filler bridging the spaces. Also, the ruffled edge of the vase top seems to have been cased where old vases are not. It is a shame current makers put these pieces on the market without markings and only close attention by the buyer will prevent the collector from buying new for old.

Twigs (Reproduction)

Price Guide

This price guide has been expanded to include in a complete, up-to-date manner, both American and English opalescent glass production from 1890 to 1930. This is a natural time frame for such glass and sets a distinctive break between antique glassware and contemporary production. Designed to supply prices for virtually all shapes and colors catalogued in this 40 year period, I know of no other reference that can duplicate this work. Prices followed by an asterisk (*) are speculative. The same mark (*) after a pattern name indicates this pattern has been reproduced in some shape(s). In a few instances, prices have been averaged where several varieties of a shape exist, but I have made a concerted effort to list prices as completely as possible.

Values were determined and tabulated from dealer's lists, shop taggings, antique guide listings, and personal speculation. Auction prices played only a minor role due to their often inflated bidding value. All items are priced as *mint* in condition and without flaw or color poorness, as well as being complete (American sugars have lids, British sugars are open compote shapes). *Please remember this is only a guide and prices herein are not set in stone. As with all guides it is meant to advise rather than set prices.*

Most pattern names conform to those used by William Heacock except where another name is more commonly accepted. In such cases I've included both names for reference.

I welcome comments from all collectors, but do ask that anyone who wants a reply, please include a self-addressed, stamped envelope with your correspondence. I especially encourage those letters that include information I have not had for this book; for this is how I learn and how my books improve with each edition.

	Blue	Green	White	Vaseline/Canary	Cranberry	Other	
Abalone							
Bowl	35.00	30.00	26.00	39.00			
Acorn Burrs (& Bark)							
Bowl, sauce	55.00		40.00				
Adonis Pineapple							
Claret bottle	365.00					395.00	Amber
Alaska							
Pitcher	395.00		350.00	375.00		450.00	Emerald
Tumbler	75.00		60.00	75.00		85.00	Emerald
Butter	390.00		295.00	400.00		290.00	Emerald
Sugar w/lid	170.00		140.00	165.00		165.00	Emerald
Creamer	90.00		70.00	85.00		80.00	Emerald
Spooner	90.00		70.00	85.00		80.00	Emerald
Bowl, Master	175.00		140.00	175.00		165.00	Emerald
Bowl, Sauce	65.00		30.00	60.00		60.00	Emerald
Cruet	300.00		260.00	290.00		285.00	Emerald
Tray	200.00		140.00	190.00		175.00	Emerald
Banana Boat	275.00		255.00	275.00		270.00	Emerald
Shakers, pair	150.00		75.00	140.00		95.00	Emerald
Bride's Basket	295.00		150.00				
Alhambra							
Rose Bowl	150.00		120.00	160.00	275.00		
Syrup	375.00		290.00	390.00	575.00		
Tumbler	70.00		50.00	65.00	115.00		
Alva							
Oil lamp	250.00*		220.00*				
Arabian Nights							
Pitcher	400.00		300.00	400.00	950.00		
Tumbler	75.00		50.00	70.00	120.00		
Syrup	250.00		195.00	275.00			
Argonaut Shell* (Nautilus)							
Pitcher	495.00		365.00				
Tumbler	120.00		95.00	100.00			
Butter	310.00		260.00				
Sugar	250.00		210.00				
Creamer	200.00		160.00				
Spooner	200.00		145.00				
Bowl, Master	150.00		120.00				
Bowl, Sauce	65.00		50.00				
Cruet	500.00		350.00				
Shakers, pair	100.00		75.00	85.00			
Jelly Compote	100.00		70.00	80.00			

	Blue	Green	White	Vaseline/ Canary	Cranberry	Other
Novety Bowls	65.00		45.00	95.00		
Add 15% for Script signed pieces						
Arched Panels						
Bowl, master				90.00		
Bowl, sauce				30.00		
Argus (Thumbprint)						
Compote	85.00		45.00	75.00		
Ascot						
Bowl	60.00			75.00		
Creamer	85.00			90.00		
Open Sugar	80.00			85.00		
Biscuit Jar	175.00			155.00		
Astro						
Bowl	55.00	50.00	40.00	50.00		
Hat Whimsey	70.00	70.00	60.00	75.00		
Aurora Borealis						
Novelty Vase	65.00	80.00	50.00			
Autumn Leaves						
Bowl	60.00	75.00	45.00			
Banana Bowl	70.00	95.00	50.00			
Baby Coinspot*						
Syrup			135.00			
Vase		95.00		85.00		
Ball Foot Hobnail						
Bowl			75.00			
Band and Rib (Threaded Optic)						
Rose Bowl	55.00		40.00			
Bowl, 7" – 9"	40.00		30.00			
Banded Neck Scale Optic						
Vase			50.00			
Barbells						
Bowl	40.00	50.00	30.00	45.00		
Basketweave* (Open Edge)						
Console Set, 3 pcs.	240.00	260.00	190.00	250.00		
Nappy	50.00	40.00	37.00	45.00		
Bowl	45.00	40.00	35.00	40.00		
Plate	90.00	100.00	65.00	125.00		

	Blue	Green	White	Vaseline/ Canary	Cranberry	Other
Beaded Base Jip						
Vase	65.00		40.00			
Beaded Block						
Creamer			65.00			
Sugar			75.00			
Beaded Cable						
Bowl, Footed	50.00	40.00	30.00	46.00		
Rose Bowl, Footed	65.00	57.00	45.00	60.00		
Beaded Drapes						
Bowl, Footed	45.00	40.00	35.00	55.00		
Banana Bowl, Footed						
Rose Bowl, Footed	50.00	45.00	40.00	60.00		
Beaded Fan						
Bowl, Footed	40.00	45.00	36.00			
Rose Bowl, Footed	50.00	50.00	42.00			
Beaded Fleur De Lis						
Compote	50.00	50.00	40.00			
Rose Bowl	55.00	55.00	47.00			
Bowl, Novelty	50.00	50.00	40.00			
Bowl Whimsey	85.00	90.00	70.00			
Beaded Moon & Stars						
Bowl	70.00		50.00			
Compote	80.00		60.00			
Banana Bowl, stemmed	85.00		65.00			
Beaded Ovals & Holly						
Spooner	90.00		65.00	85.00		
Beaded Ovals In Sand						
Pitcher	400.00	400.00				
Tumbler	95.00	90.00				
Butter	285.00	265.00				
Sugar	225.00	225.00				
Creamer	90.00	80.00				
Spooner	90.00	80.00				
Bowl, Master	75.00	70.00				
Bowl, Sauce	35.00	30.00				
Cruet	240.00	225.00				
Shakers, pair	100.00	90.00				
Toothpick Holder	200.00	190.00				
Nappy	55.00	45.00				
Beaded Star Medallion						
Shade	65.00	55.00	45.00			

	Blue	Green	White	Vaseline/ Canary	Cranberry	Other
Beaded Stars & Swag						
Plate	95.00					
Bowl	45.00	55.00	37.00			
Rose Bowl	60.00	60.00	42.00			
Advertising Bowl	420.00	450.00	300.00			
Advertising Plate	510.00	55.00	450.00			
Beads & Bark						
Vase, footed	75.00	70.00	60.00			
Beads & Curleycues						
Novelty Bowls, ftd.	48.00	46.00	40.00			
(Beatty) Honeycomb*						
Pitcher	195.00		150.00			
Tumbler	60.00		40.00			
Sugar	120.00		90.00			
Creamer	100.00		60.00			
Spooner	90.00		60.00			
Bowl, Master	55.00		45.00			
Bowl, Sauce	30.00		25.00			
Cruet	200.00		175.00			
Toothpick Holder	250.00		225.00			
Celery Vase	85.00		75.00			
Shakers, pair	80.00		65.00			
Mustard Pot	100.00		80.00			
Mug	55.00		40.00			
Individual cream/sugar set	165.00		135.00			
Butter	200.00		160.00			
Beatty Rib						
Pitcher	185.00		140.00			
Tumbler	50.00		35.00			
Butter	200.00		115.00			
Sugar	135.00		95.00			
Creamer	65.00		40.00			
Spooner	65.00		40.00			
Bowl, Master	55.00		35.00			
Bowl, Sauce	30.00		20.00			
Celery Vase	80.00		70.00			
Mug	55.00		40.00			
Ashtray, Cigar	85.00*					
Mustard Jar	150.00		110.00			
Nappy, various	40.00		30.00			
Shakers, pair	75.00		60.00			
Salt Dip	60.00		45.00			
Cracker Jar	120.00		90.00			
Sugar Shaker	125.00		100.00			
Finger Bowl	35.00		25.00			

	Blue	Green	White	Vaseline/ Canary	Cranberry	Other	
Match Holder	50.00		35.00				
Toothpick	65.00		55.00				
Bowl Novelty 9"	75.00		65.00				
Beatty Swirl							
Pitcher	180.00		120.00	190.00			
Tumbler	40.00		35.00	50.00			
Butter	170.00		150.00				
Sugar	130.00		90.00				
Creamer	75.00		60.00				
Spooner	75.00		60.00				
Bowl, Master	55.00		40.00				
Bowl, Sauce	30.00		21.00				
Celery Vase	80.00		60.00				
Mug	60.00		40.00	80.00			
Syrup	240.00		190.00	250.00			
Water Tray	90.00		70.00	95.00			
Berry Patch							
Novelty Bowl	50.00	45.00	35.00				
Blackberry							
Nappy	40.00	45.00	30.00			55.00	Amethyst
Plate 6"			65.00			85.00	Amethyst
Bon-bon			50.00			75.00	Amethyst
Bowl			30.00			65.00	Amethyst
Blackberry Spray							
Hat			40.00			90.00	Amethyst
Blocked Thumbprint & Beads							
(Fishscale & Beads)							
Bowl	50.00	55.00	40.00				
Nappy	40.00	40.00	30.00				
Blooms & Blossoms							
Nappy, Handled	50.00	50.00	40.00				
Proof Whimsey	95.00						
Blossom & Palms							
Bowl	47.00	45.00	36.00				
Blossom & Web							
Bowl	170.00	175.00	145.00				
Blown Diamonds							
Pitcher				300.00*			
(Blown) Drape							
Pitcher	550.00	500.00	350.00		900.00		

	Blue	Green	White	Vaseline/ Canary	Cranberry	Other
Tumbler	185.00	175.00	155.00		315.00	
Sugar Shaker	500.00	450.00	300.00			
(Blown) Twist						
Pitcher	550.00	500.00	350.00	525.00	900.00	
Tumbler	185.00	175.00	155.00	175.00	315.00	
Sugar Shaker	195.00	185.00	170.00	185.00	575.00	
Syrup	250.00		190.00		380.00	
Celery Vase			350.00	450.00		
Boggy Bayou						
Vase	40.00	37.00	30.00			60.00 Amethyst
Brideshead						
Pitcher, 2 sizes	145.00*					
Tumbler	90.00*					
Butter	95.00					
Sugar	70.00					
Creamer	65.00					
Celery Vase	60.00					
Novelty Bowl	50.00					
Oval Tray, 10"	110.00		100.00	115.00		
Broken Pillar						
Compote	60.00			55.00		
Card Tray	70.00			65.00		
(from compote shape)						
(Bubble) Lattice						
Pitcher, various	270.00	260.00	210.00	265.00	750.00	
Tumbler, various	50.00	50.00	40.00	45.00	110.00	
Butter	200.00	180.00	145.00	195.00	700.00	
Sugar	100.00	80.00	70.00	95.00	420.00	
Creamer	60.00	50.00	50.00	55.00	150.00	
Spooner	60.00	50.00	50.00	55.00	195.00	
Bowl, Master	70.00	50.00	45.00	65.00	80.00	
Sauce	30.00	25.00	20.00	30.00	35.00	
Cruet, avg. pricing	175.00	160.00	135.00	170.00	400.00	
Syrup, various	200.00	180.00	160.00	190.00	750.00	
Sugar Shaker	225.00	210.00	185.00	215.00	290.00	
Toothpick holder	300.00	265.00	190.00	350.00	280.00 – 540.00	
Bride's Basket	120.00	95.00	70.00	125.00	225.00	
Finger Bowl	45.00	40.00	25.00	45.00	110.00	
Shakers, various	150.00	125.00	100.00	175.00	150.00 – 300.00	
Celery Vase					120.00	
Bulbous Base Coinspot						
Sugar Shaker	120.00		90.00		165.00	

	Blue	Green	White	Vaseline/ Canary	Cranberry	Other
Bull's Eye						
Bowl	50.00				65.00	
Water Bottle			160.00		250.00	
Shade	60.00		40.00			
Bushel Basket						
One shape, scarce	150.00	325.00	90.00	350.00		
Button Panels						
Bowl	45.00		35.00	50.00		
Rose Bowl	45.00		37.00	55.00		
Buttons & Braids						
Pitcher	180.00	170.00	125.00	275.00*	395.00	
Tumbler	45.00	40.00	30.00	80.00*	90.00	
Bowl	50.00	55.00	35.00		85.00	
Cabbage Leaf						
Novelty, Footed Bowl	80.00	65.00	50.00			
Calyx						
Vase	65.00		50.00	60.00		
Carousel						
Bowl	55.00	50.00	37.00			
Cane & Diamond Swirl						
Stemmed Tray	75.00			70.00		
Casbah						
Compote			150.00*			
Cashews						
Bowl	50.00	47.00	30.00			
Rose Bowl	100.00	95.00	75.00			
Whimsey Bowl	55.00	52.00	38.00			
Cherry						
Master Bowl	65.00					
Small Bowl	30.00					
Covered Butter	200.00					
Creamer	110.00					
Sugar	120.00					
Spooner	110.00					
Goblet	70.00					
Wine	75.00					
Plate, Rare	150.00					
Open Compote	90.00					
Covered Compote	120.00					
Novelty Bowls	60.00					

	Blue	Green	White	Vaseline/ Canary	Cranberry	Other	
Cherry Panels							
Novelty Bowl	75.00		60.00	70.00			
Chippendale							
Compote	65.00			75.00			
Basket	60.00			60.00			
Pitcher	120.00			135.00			
Tumbler	35.00			30.00			
Christmas Pearls							
Cruet	295.00	275.00	350.00*				
Shakers, pair	150.00	135.00	175.00*				
Christmas Snowflake*							
Pitcher, either	675.00		500.00		950.00		
Tumbler, average	110.00		90.00		125.00		
Chrysanthemum							
Ftd bowl, 11"	250.00		150.00			300.00	Amethyst
Chrysanthemum Base Swirl							
Pitcher	395.00		345.00		850.00		
Tumbler	90.00		70.00		120.00		
Butter	325.00		295.00		500.00		
Sugar	200.00		175.00		350.00		
Creamer	95.00		70.00		395.00		
Spooner	95.00		70.00		200.00		
Bowl, Master	55.00		45.00		120.00		
Bowl, Sauce	35.00		30.00		50.00		
Cruet	225.00		175.00		475.00		
Syrup	200.00		175.00		495.00		
Sugar Shaker	200.00		175.00		265.00		
Toothpick Holder	95.00		70.00		300.00		
Shakers, pair	125.00		100.00		295.00		
Finger Bowl	45.00		35.00		140.00		
Celery Vase	135.00		110.00		200.00		
Straw Holder w/lid	500.00		400.00		1,200.00		
Mustard Pot	150.00		120.00		225.00		
Chrysanthemum Swirl Variant							
Pitcher, rare	375.00		265.00		900.00	400.00	Teal
Tumbler, rare	90.00		60.00		100.00		
Circled Scroll							
Pitcher	475.00	425.00	400.00				
Tumbler	90.00	85.00	70.00				
Butter	465.00	350.00	295.00				
Sugar	250.00	225.00	200.00				
Creamer	175.00	165.00	125.00				
Spooner	175.00	165.00	125.00				

	Blue	Green	White	Vaseline/ Canary	Cranberry	Other	
Bowl, Master	165.00	150.00	120.00				
Bowl, Sauce	55.00	50.00	40.00				
Cruet	695.00	675.00	450.00				
Shakers, pair	300.00	295.00	245.00				
Jelly Compote	150.00	140.00	125.00				

Cleopatra's Fan (Northwood Shell)

	Blue	Green	White				
Vase, novelty	65.00	75.00					

Coin Dot Chevron Base

	Blue		White				
Oil Lamp	300.00*		225.00*				

Coin Dot (Inverted Thumbprint Base)

	Blue		White				
Lamp	300.00*		200.00*				

Coinspot* (includes variants — prices averaged)

	Blue	Green	White	Vaseline/ Canary	Cranberry	Other	
Pitcher	260.00	245.00	165.00	190.00	390.00	200.00	Rubina
Tumbler	40.00	35.00	30.00	36.00	90.00	75.00	Rubina
Bowl, Master	47.00	40.00	30.00		70.00		
Bowl, Sauce	30.00	25.00	18.00		40.00		
Syrup	165.00	150.00	135.00		395.00	300.00	Rubina
Cruet, various	250.00	230.00	100.00	240.00	375.00	400.00	Rubina
Shakers, each	135.00	95.00	70.00	90.00	195.00		
Compote	60.00	45.00	40.00				
Sugar Shaker	100.00	95.00	75.00	100.00	375.00	250.00	Rubina
Novelty Bowls	60.00	55.00	40.00		75.00		
Celery Vase	125.00	110.00	90.00	120.00	175.00		
Tumble-up	150.00	140.00	120.00		275.00		
Toothpick Holder	265.00	250.00	140.00	230.00	275.00	295.00	Rubina
Barber Bottle	175.00	170.00	130.00		300.00		
Pickle Castor	295.00		200.00		750.00		
Lamp (from syrup)	295.00		240.00		900.00		
Perfume	65.00	75.00	60.00				

Colonial Stairsteps

	Blue						
Creamer	100.00						
Sugar	100.00						
Toothpick Holder	195.00						

Compass

	Blue	Green					
Plate, rare	250.00	225.00					
Bowl, scarce	150.00	150.00					

Concave Columns

	Blue		White	Vaseline/ Canary			
Vase	100.00		75.00	95.00			

	Blue	Green	White	Vaseline/ Canary	Cranberry	Other	
Consolidated Criss-Cross							
Pitcher			550.00		950.00		
Tumbler			100.00		115.00		
Sugar			325.00		365.00		
Butter			425.00		725.00		
Creamer			250.00		365.00		
Spooner			225.00		285.00		
Bowl, Master			110.00		185.00		
Bowl, Sauce			50.00		70.00		
Shakers, each			90.00		100.00	165.00	Rubina
Cruet			275.00		795.00		
Sugar Shaker			310.00		550.00	660.00	Rubina
Syrup			325.00		825.00	700.00	Rubina
Finger Bowl			90.00		120.00		
Celery Vase			135.00		175.00		
Mustard Pot			150.00		195.00		
Toothpick Holder			195.00		500.00		
Ivy Ball			300.00*		700.00		
Constellation (Seafoam)							
Compote	275.00		200.00				
Contessa							
Basket, Handled	60.00			75.00		250.00	Amber
Pitcher	125.00					325.00	Amber
Breakfast Set, ftd., 2 pc.	155.00					350.00	Amber
Coral							
Bowl	45.00	40.00	30.00	40.00			
Coral Reef							
Bitters Bottle	195.00		120.00		300.00		
Barber Bottle	190.00		120.00		295.00		
Finger Bowl	165.00		100.00		200.00		
Mini Nightlamp	500.00		385.00		1,900.00		
Oil lamp, stemmed	450.00		325.00		1,750.00		
Finger Lamp, fit	400.00		300.00		1,650.00		
Finger Lamp, stmed	500.00		400.00		2,050.00		
Corn Vase*							
Fancy Vase	200.00	295.00	125.00	185.00			
Cornith							
Vase 8" – 13"	35.00		27.00				
Cornucopia							
Handled Vase	75.00		57.00				

	Blue	Green	White	Vaseline/ Canary	Cranberry	Other
Coronation						
Pitcher	195.00			185.00		
Tumbler	40.00			40.00		
Crocus						
Vase, rare	350.00*		250.00*	350.00*		
Crown Jewels						
Pitcher	195.00					
Tumbler	55.00					
Curtain Call						
Caster Set – rare					500.00	Cobalt
Curtain Optic						
Pitcher, various	200.00	200.00	150.00	185.00		
Tumbler, various	50.00	45.00	40.00	45.00		
Guest Set, 2 pc.	95.00	100.00	80.00	100.00		
Daffodils						
Pitcher	900.00	950.00	600.00	850.00	1,350.00	
Tumbler, rare	395.00	350.00	300.00	395.00	550.00	
Oil Lamp	300.00	295.00	200.00	275.00	325.00	
Vase	295.00			250.00		
Dahlia Twist						
Vase	65.00	60.00	50.00			
Epergne	350.00	340.00	300.00			
Daisy & Button						
Lifeboat				85.00		
Bun Tray				150.00		
Bowl, novelty				65.00		
Daisy & Drape						
Vase, rare				1,500.00		
Daisy & Fern*						
Pitcher, 3 shapes	290.00	285.00	190.00		300.00 – 750.00	
Tumbler	45.00	55.00	30.00		90.00	
Butter	225.00	250.00	175.00		285.00	
Sugar	100.00	120.00	75.00		250.00	
Creamer	75.00	90.00	60.00		425.00	
Vase	140.00	140.00	90.00		190.00	
Spooner	75.00	85.00	50.00		395.00	
Bowl, Master	80.00	95.00	55.00		250.00	
Bowl, Sauce	40.00	45.00	26.00		145.00	
Sugar shaker	195.00	220.00	165.00		265.00	
Syrup, various, avg.	225.00	215.00	185.00		240.00 – 540.00	
Toothpick Holder	155.00	170.00	110.00		200.00	
Shakers, pair	300.00	260.00	175.00		295.00	
Mustard Pot	95.00	110.00	75.00		150.00	

	Blue	Green	White	Vaseline/ Canary	Cranberry	Other
Cruet	200.00	175.00	135.00		510.00	
Perfume Bottle	170.00	195.00	120.00		250.00	
Night Lamp	220.00	240.00	160.00		310.00	
Pickle Caster	315.00	325.00	245.00		425.00	
Barber Bottle					495.00	
Rose Bowl					110.00	
Finger Bowl	75.00	85.00	55.00		295.00	

Daisy & Greek Key

Sauce, ftd	65.00	60.00	40.00			

Daisy & Plume

Bowl, footed	50.00	45.00	35.00			
Rosebowl, ftd.	60.00	55.00	40.00			

Daisy Block

Rowboat, 4 sizes		80.00*	70.00*			

Daisy Dear

Bowl	45.00	40.00	30.00			

Daisy In Criss-Cross

Pitcher	300.00				450.00	
Tumbler	60.00				100.00	
Syrup	265.00				475.00	

Daisy Intaglio

Basket		180.00	150.00			
Bowl		95.00	85.00			
Plate		130.00	100.00			

Daisy May (Leaf Rays)

Bon-Bon or Nappy	40.00	45.00	28.00			

Daisy Wreath

Bowl, rare	150.00*					

Dandelion

Mug, rare	700.00*					

Desert Garden

Bowl	45.00	40.00	30.00			

Diamond & Daisy

Bowl, Novelty	60.00	65.00	40.00			
Basket, Handled	90.00	95.00	60.00			

Diamond & Oval Thumbprint

Vase	40.00	45.00	30.00			

	Blue	Green	White	Vaseline/ Canary	Cranberry	Other
Diamond Maple Leaf						
Novelty, Handled	40.00	50.00	30.00	45.00		
Bowl, Handled	75.00	70.00	50.00			
Diamond Optic						
Compote	50.00		40.00			
Stemmed Cardtray	60.00		50.00			
Diamond Point						
Vase	40.00	45.00	30.00			
Diamond Point & Fleur De Lis						
Bowl, Novelty	50.00	55.00	40.00			
Nut Bowl		65.00				
Diamond Point Columns						
Vase, rare	200.00	200.00	150.00			
Diamond Spearhead						
Pitcher, either	700.00	600.00	395.00	475.00		600.00*
Tumbler	110.00	90.00	50.00	80.00		90.00*
Goblet	165.00	150.00	100.00	140.00		130.00*
Butter	500.00	575.00	395.00	495.00		450.00*
Sugar	250.00	225.00	175.00	250.00		240.00*
Creamer, various sizes	195.00	210.00	165.00	195.00		180.00*
Spooner	165.00	200.00	155.00	170.00		165.00*
Bowl, Master	175.00	180.00	110.00	165.00		135.00*
Bowl, Sauce	50.00	55.00	30.00	40.00		35.00*
Toothpick Holder	150.00	125.00	100.00	130.00		150.00*
Mug	175.00	185.00	90.00	150.00		165.00*
Syrup	650.00	700.00	550.00	625.00		750.00*
Celery Vase	250.00	250.00	150.00	250.00		240.00*
Shakers, pair	150.00	175.00	130.00	165.00		175.00*
Jelly Compote	195.00	150.00	125.00	165.00		180.00*
Cup & Saucer Set				250.00		
Tall Compote	400.00	395.00	300.00	395.00		450.00
Tall Creamer	200.00			200.00		260.00
Oil Bottle	100.00			90.00		90.00
Spittoon Whimsey		550.00		500.00		
Relish Tray			90.00	150.00		
Plate, 10"	160.00			140.00		
Water Carafe	250.00		175.00	200.00		
Mini Creamer	200.00	200.00	150.00	200.00		225.00 Sapphire
Diamond Stem						
Vase 6½"	175.00	190.00	90.00	170.00		100.00 Aqua
Vase 8½"	150.00	175.00	85.00	145.00		

*Emerald or Sapphire

	Blue	Green	White	Vaseline/ Canary	Cranberry	Other	
Diamond Wave							
Pitcher w/Lid					165.00	250.00	Amethyst
Tumbler					40.00		
Vase 5"					75.00		
Diamonds							
Pitcher, 2 shapes					400.00	275.00	Rubina
Cruet					350.00		
Vase, 6" decorated			75.00				
Dogwood Drape							
Compote	150.00*		120.00*				
Dolly Madison							
Pitcher	395.00	400.00	310.00				
Tumbler	80.00	95.00	60.00				
Butter	325.00	350.00	275.00				
Sugar	150.00	160.00	110.00				
Creamer	90.00	100.00	75.00				
Spooner	80.00	90.00	60.00				
Bowl, Master	60.00	70.00	55.00				
Bowl, Sauce	30.00	35.00	25.00				
Plate 6", scarce	110.00	110.00	70.00				
Bowl, Novelty	60.00	70.00	50.00				
Dolphin*							
Compote	65.00		45.00	60.00			
Dolphin & Herons							
Compote, Footed Novelty	195.00		180.00	220.00			
Tray, Footed Novelty	190.00		175.00				
Dolphin Petticoat							
Candlestick, each	175.00		125.00	165.00			
Double Dolphin (1533)							
Compote, rare	150.00		100.00				
Double Greek Key							
Pitcher	375.00		325.00				
Tumbler	80.00		65.00				
Butter	300.00		250.00				
Sugar	175.00		140.00				
Creamer	100.00		75.00				
Spooner	100.00		75.00				
Bowl, Master	75.00		60.00				
Bowl, Sauce	40.00		30.00				
Celery Vase	165.00		135.00				
Pickle Tray	150.00		95.00				
Shakers, pair	225.00		185.00				
Mustard Pot	200.00		155.00				
Toothpick Holder	250.00		195.00				

	Blue	Green	White	Vaseline/Canary	Cranberry	Other
Double Stemmed Rose						
Bowl, very rare	250.00	200.00	150.00			
Dragon & Lotus						
Bowl, rare			300.00			
Dragon Lady (Diamond Compass)						
Rose Bowl	160.00	150.00	90.00			
Novelty Bowl	140.00	130.00	90.00			
Vase	95.00	90.00	60.00			
Drapery, Northwood's						
Pitcher	250.00		220.00			
Tumbler	70.00		55.00			
Butter	195.00		175.00			
Sugar	135.00		120.00			
Creamer	90.00		80.00			
Spooner	80.00		70.00			
Bowl, Master	110.00		75.00			
Bowl, Sauce	40.00		30.00			
Rose Bowl	90.00		75.00			
Vase	175.00	190.00	155.00	170.00		
Duchess						
Pitcher	175.00		150.00	175.00		
Tumbler	35.00		27.00	30.00		
Butter	175.00		150.00	165.00		
Sugar	100.00		80.00	100.00		
Creamer	65.00		45.00	60.00		
Spooner	65.00		50.00	65.00		
Bowl, Master	95.00		65.00	80.00		
Bowl, Sauce	35.00		25.00	30.00		
Toothpick Holder	150.00		115.00	150.00		
Cruet	200.00		160.00	195.00		
Lampshade	95.00		75.00			
Dugan Intaglio Grape						
Plate, 12½", rare			250.00			
Bowl			125.00			
Compote			85.00			
Dugan Jack-in-the-Pulpit						
Vase, 4½"	50.00	50.00	35.00			
Hex Base Vase, 7½"	60.00	70.00	40.00			
(floral etched – add 15%)						
Dugan Peach Intaglio						
Plate, 13"			185.00			
Bowl			95.00			
Compote			95.00			

	Blue	Green	White	Vaseline/ Canary	Cranberry	Other
Dugan's #1013 (Wide Rib)						
Vase	65.00	75.00	50.00			
Bowl Whimsey	50.00	55.00	40.00			
Dugan's Olive Nappy						
one shape	45.00	40.00	30.00			
Ellen						
Vase	50.00	55.00	40.00			
Ellipse & Diamond						
Pitcher					500.00*	
Tumbler					115.00*	
English Drape						
Vase	60.00		40.00	60.00		
English Spool						
Vase				65.00		
Estate						
Vase	65.00	85.00	40.00			
Everglades						
Pitcher	460.00			495.00		
Tumbler	85.00			90.00		
Butter	360.00			375.00		
Sugar	195.00			200.00		
Creamer	150.00			150.00		
Spooner	150.00			150.00		
Oval Bowl, Master	185.00			195.00		
Oval Bowl, Sauce	40.00			40.00		
Cruet	475.00			495.00		
Shakers, pair	275.00			280.00		
Jelly Compote	140.00	165.00		140.00		
Everglades (Cambridge)						
Compote			60.00			
Fan						
Pitcher	295.00	290.00	200.00			
Tumbler	35.00	30.00	20.00			
Butter	395.00	385.00	220.00			
Sugar	200.00	185.00	150.0			
Creamer	120.00	110.00	85.00			
Spooner	120.00	110.00	85.00			
Bowl, Sauce	30.00	30.00	25.00			
Bowl, Maste	75.00	70.00	65.00			
Gravy Boat	45.00	48.00	40.00			
Novelty Bowls	40.00	40.00	30.00			
Whimsey Bowls	50.00	50.00	40.00			
Fancy Fantails						
Bowl	40.00	45.00	25.00	40.00		
Rose Bowl	45.00	50.00	30.00	45.00		

	Blue	Green	White	Vaseline/ Canary	Cranberry	Other
Feathers						
Vase	35.00	32.00	26.00			
Whimsey Bowl, rare			100.00*			
Whimsey Nut Bowl, rare	150.00	150.00				
Fenton #100						
Bowl				50.00		55.00 Amethyst
Fenton #220 (Stripe)						
Pitcher w/lid	240.00	230.00	170.00	225.00		
Tumbler, Handled	28.00	32.00	18.00	25.00		
Tumble-up, Complete	150.00	140.00	90.00	135.00		
Fenton #370						
Bowl						45.00 Amber
Vase						50.00 Amber
Nappy						55.00 Amber
Bon-bon						50.00 Amber
Fenton #950						
Cornucopia Candlestick, each						95.00 Amethyst
Fenton Drapery						
Pitcher	420.00*	400.00*	290.00*			
Tumbler	65.00*	55.00*	40.00*			
Fern						
Pitcher, various	250.00		175.00		700.00 – 800.00	
Tumbler	45.00		40.00		100.00	
Butter	250.00		220.00		375.00	
Sugar	200.00		170.00		230.00	
Bowl, Master	100.00		75.00		125.00	
Bowl, Sauce	50.00		35.00		55.00	
Sugar Shaker, various	100.00		75.00		525.00	
Syrup	275.00		200.00		595.00	
Cruet	200.00		200.00		495.00	
Shakers, pair	160.00		100.00		150.00	
Celery Vase	125.00		90.00		145.00	
Mustard Pot	140.00		115.00		165.00	
Toothpick Holder, rare	350.00		190.00		400.00 – 500.00	
Finger Bowl	65.00		45.00		100.00	
Barber Bottle	150.00		100.00		295.00	
Creamer	125.00		90.00		150.00	
Spooner	125.00		90.00		140.00	
Fine Rib						
Vase, rare				400.00*		
Finecut & Roses						
Rose Bowl, rare	65.00	75.00	50.00			
Novelty Bowls	45.00	50.00	40.00			
Fish In The Sea						
Vase	375.00	425.00	285.00	600.00*		
Vase Whimsey	95.00	90.00	70.00			

	Blue	Green	White	Vaseline/ Canary	Cranberry	Other	
Fishnet							
Epergne	165.00		125.00			185.00	Emerald
(one shape, 2 pc.)							
Fishscale & Beads							
Bowl	40.00		28.00				
Flora							
Pitcher	495.00		400.00	475.00			
Tumbler	85.00		60.00	80.00			
Butter	275.00		175.00	250.00			
Sugar	135.00		100.00	125.00			
Creamer	100.00		75.00	90.00			
Spooner	100.00		90.00	100.00			
Bowl, Master	100.00		75.00	95.00			
Bowl, Sauce	50.00		30.00	40.00			
Cruet	750.00		450.00	600.00			
Toothpick Holder	475.00		300.00	400.00			
Syrup	400.00		300.00	395.00			
Shakers, pair	395.00		295.00	375.00			
Jelly Compote	150.00		110.00	140.00			
Celery Vase	125.00		90.00	100.00			
Novelty Bowl	65.00		40.00	55.00			
Floral Eyelet*							
Pitcher	500.00*		400.00*		850.00*		
Tumbler	100.00*		85.00*		250.00*		
Fluted Bars & Beads							
Rose Bowl	50.00	45.00	40.00	60.00			
Novelty Bowl	55.00	50.00	45.00	65.00			
Vase Novelty	60.00	55.00	50.00	70.00			
Fluted Scrolls (Klondyke)*							
Pitcher	240.00		165.00	200.00			
Tumbler	90.00		40.00	75.00			
Butter	175.00		150.00	170.00			
Sugar	130.00		90.00	100.00			
Spooner	75.00		50.00	60.00			
Creamer	75.00		50.00	70.00			
Bowl, Master	75.00		55.00	70.00			
Bowl, Sauce	30.00		25.00	30.00			
Cruet	185.00		160.00	175.00			
Shakers, pair	95.00		70.00	80.00			
Epergne, small	120.00		90.00	125.00			
Rose Bowl	135.00		85.00	120.00			
Novelty Bowl	50.00		40.00	50.00			
Puff Box	65.00		50.00	60.00			

Note: A variant called Fluted Scrolls with Flower Band is priced the same as above.

	Blue	Green	White	Vaseline/ Canary	Cranberry	Other	
Fluted Scrolls With Vine							
Vase, Footed	75.00		45.00	85.00			

	Blue	Green	White	Vaseline/ Canary	Cranberry	Other	
Footed Shell							
Novelty Piece, rare		400.00*					
Forked Strip							
Barber Bottle			275.00*				
Four Pillars							
Vase	65.00	70.00	45.00	60.00			
Frosted Leaf & Basketweave							
Butter	275.00		200.00	250.00			
Sugar	175.00		150.00	160.00			
Creamer	150.00		130.00	135.00			
Spooner	140.00		110.00	120.00			
Gonterman (Adonis) Hob							
Cruet						425.00	Amber
Gonterman (Adonis) Swirl							
Pitcher	400.00					375.00	Amber
Tumbler	90.00					75.00	Amber
Butter	390.00					340.00	Amber
Sugar	250.00					210.00	Amber
Creamer	175.00					125.00	Amber
Spooner	150.00					120.00	Amber
Bowl, Master	95.00					85.00	Amber
Bowl, Sauce	50.00					50.00	Amber
Cruet	400.00					375.00	Amber
Celery Vase	210.00					195.00	Amber
Syrup	400.00					375.00	Amber
Shade	100.00					100.00	Amber
Toothpick Holder	300.00					195.00	Amber
Gossamer Threads							
Bowl	40.00						
Fingerbowl	50.00						
Plate, 6"	65.00						
Grape & Cable							
Centerpiece Bowl	275.00	265.00	200.00	245.00			
Bon-Bon				400.00			
Fruit Bowl, lg	275.00	265.00	225.00	250.00			
Grape & Cherry							
Bowl	70.00	90.00	55.00	80.00			
Grape & Vine							
JIP Vase	50.00						
Grapevine Cluster							
Vase, Footed	165.00		100.00	150.00			
Grecian Urn							
Vase 4½" tall	60.00						
Greek Key & Ribs							
Bowl	60.00	55.00	40.00				

	Blue	Green	White	Vaseline/Canary	Cranberry	Other
Greek Key & Scales						
Novelty Bowl	85.00	75.00	60.00			
Harrow						
Creamer	75.00			70.00		
Open Sugar	70.00			65.00		
Wine, Stemmed	40.00			40.00		
Cordial, Stemmed	35.00			37.00		
Heart-Handle Open O's						
Ring Tray	95.00	85.00	65.00			
Hearts & Clubs						
Bowl, Footed	55.00	50.00	40.00			
Hearts & Flowers						
Bowl	75.00		60.00			
Compote	350.00		300.00			
Heatherbloom						
Vase	35.00	32.00	20.00			
Herringbone						
Pitcher	575.00		475.00		725.00	
Tumbler	100.00		60.00		150.00	
Cruet	295.00		220.00		685.00	
Heron & Peacock*						
Mug	70.00		60.00			
Hilltop Vines						
Novelty Chalice	65.00	60.00	40.00			
Hobnail & Panelled Thumbprint						
Pitcher	300.00		150.00	275.00		
Tumbler	75.00		45.00	65.00		
Butter	185.00		140.00	170.00		
Sugar	115.00		90.00	85.00		
Creamer	85.00		60.00	65.00		
Spooner	85.00		65.00	70.00		
Bowl, Master	75.00		60.00	65.00		
Bowl, Sauce	35.00		26.00	32.00		
Hobnail, Hobbs						
Pitcher , 5 Sizes	250.00 – 350.00		150.00 – 250.00	200.00 – 300.00	350.00 – 550.00	250.00 – 400.00 Rubina
Tumbler	70.00		50.00	70.00		100.00 Rubina
Butter	275.00		190.00	225.00		
Sugar	200.00		135.00	165.00		
Creamer	90.00		100.00	95.00		
Spooner	90.00		100.00	95.00		
Bowl, Master, square	90.00		75.00	95.00		
Bowl, Sauce, square	35.00		30.00	30.00		
Cruet	200.00		200.00	190.00		
Syrup	225.00		200.00	210.00		350.00 Rubina
Finger Bowl	65.00		50.00	55.00		
Barber Bottle	145.00		125.00	130.00		

	Blue	Green	White	Vaseline/Canary	Cranberry	Other	
Celery Vase	160.00		120.00	100.00		225.00	Rubina
Water Tray	175.00		110.00	140.00			
Bride's Basket	450.00			410.00	500.00	500.00	Rubina
Lemonade Set, Complete	600.00				700.00		
Shaker, each			200.00		400.00		

Hobnail, Northwood's

	Blue	Green	White	Vaseline/Canary	Cranberry	Other	
Pitcher			100.00				
Tumbler			30.00				
Butter			130.00				
Sugar			100.00				
Creamer			60.00				
Spooner			60.00				
Bowl, Master			55.00				
Bowl, Sauce			30.00				
Mug			85.00				
Celery Vase			95.00				
Breakfast Set, 2 piece set			135.00				

Hobnail 4-Footed

	Blue	Green	White	Vaseline/Canary	Cranberry	Other	
Butter			155.00	175.00		210.00	Cobalt
Sugar			80.00	110.00		135.00	Cobalt
Creamer			70.00	85.00		90.00	Cobalt
Spooner			70.00	85.00		90.00	Cobalt

Hobnail In Square*

	Blue	Green	White	Vaseline/Canary	Cranberry	Other	
Pitcher			220.00				
Tumbler			35.00				
Butter			185.00				
Sugar			130.00				
Creamer			100.00				
Spooner			90.00				
Bowl, Master			70.00				
Bowl, Sauce			27.00				
Celery Vase			130.00				
Shakers, pair			90.00				
Compote, various			95.00				
Barber Bottle			120.00				
Bowl, with stand	150.00		100.00				

Holly

	Blue	Green	White	Vaseline/Canary	Cranberry	Other	
Bowl			75.00				

Holly & Berry

	Blue	Green	White	Vaseline/Canary	Cranberry	Other	
Nappy, rare			275.00				

Honeycomb

	Blue	Green	White	Vaseline/Canary	Cranberry	Other	
Vase	75.00*	90.00	50.00				

Honeycomb & Clover

	Blue	Green	White	Vaseline/Canary	Cranberry	Other	
Pitcher	395.00	350.00	275.00				
Tumbler	100.00	80.00	60.00				
Butter	365.00	350.00	270.00				

	Blue	Green	White	Vaseline/ Canary	Cranberry	Other	
Sugar	290.00	275.00	145.00				
Creamer	150.00	140.00	110.00				
Spooner	150.00	140.00	110.00				
Bowl, Master	85.00	80.00	60.00				
Bowl, Sauce	40.00	35.00	30.00				
Bowl, Novelty	70.00	70.00	60.00				

Honeycomb (Blown)

	Blue	Green	White	Vaseline/ Canary	Cranberry	Other	
Pitcher	300.00		210.00		475.00	425.00	Amber
Tumbler	75.00		45.00		90.00	65.00	Amber
Cracker Jar	310.00		245.00		395.00	400.00	Amber
Syrup	295.00		270.00		410.00	450.00	Amber
Barber Bottle	170.00		110.00		170.00	190.00	Amber

Horse Chestnut

	Blue	Green	White	Vaseline/ Canary	Cranberry	Other
Blown Vase				95.00*		

Idyll

	Blue	Green	White	Vaseline/ Canary	Cranberry	Other
Pitcher	375.00	360.00	300.00			
Tumbler	90.00	85.00	70.00			
Butter	350.00	370.00	295.00			
Sugar	170.00	195.00	150.00			
Creamer	140.00	130.00	80.00			
Spooner	140.00	130.00	75.00			
Bowl, Master	60.00	60.00	40.00			
Bowl, Sauce	30.00	30.00	20.00			
Toothpick Holder	395.00	310.00	270.00			
Cruet	210.00	200.00	170.00			
Shakers, pair	115.00	100.00	90.00			
Tray	120.00	110.00	90.00			
Bowl, 6" – 7"	40.00	45.00	30.00			

Inside Ribbing

	Blue	Green	White	Vaseline/ Canary	Cranberry	Other
Bowl, Master	65.00		40.00	75.00		
Bowl, Sauce	30.00		20.00	35.00		
Butter	225.00		150.00	240.00		
Sugar	110.00		90.00	120.00		
Spooner	75.00		60.00	80.00		
Creamer	75.00		60.00	80.00		
Pitcher	275.00		160.00	280.00		
Tumbler	60.00		30.00	65.00		
Celery Vase	55.00		35.00	60.00		
Syrup	150.00		95.00	140.00		
Jelly Compote	65.00		30.00	60.00		
Toothpick Holder	200.00		160.00	195.00		
Cruet	135.00		90.00	130.00		
Shakers, pair	100.00		70.00	90.00		
Tray	50.00		30.00	50.00		
Rose Bowl	75.00					

Intaglio

	Blue	Green	White	Vaseline/ Canary	Cranberry	Other
Pitcher	225.00		135.00			
Tumbler	110.00		65.00			

	Blue	Green	White	Vaseline/ Canary	Cranberry	Other	
Butter	485.00		260.00				
Sugar	160.00		95.00				
Creamer	85.00		50.00				
Spooner	90.00		60.00				
Bowl, Master, Ftd.	220.00		90.00	240.00			
Bowl, Sauce, Ftd.	35.00		20.00	45.00			
Shakers, pair	95.00		75.00				
Jelly Compote	60.00		45.00	75.00			
Novelty Bowl	50.00		30.00	65.00			
Cruet	195.00		140.00	300.00*			

Intaglio, Dugan's

	Blue	Green	White	Vaseline/ Canary	Cranberry	Other	
Bowl, 7" – 10"			120.00				
Compote, 5" – 7"			100.00				
Compote, 8" – 11"			150.00				
Nappy, 6" – 9"			75.00				
Plate, 11"			135.00				

Note: These items are all goofus on crystal with opalescent treatment

Interior Panel

	Blue	Green	White	Vaseline/ Canary	Cranberry	Other	
Fan Vase	55.00	50.00	35.00	55.00		75.00	Amber
						80.00	Amethyst

Interior Swirl

	Blue	Green	White	Vaseline/ Canary	Cranberry	Other	
Rose Bowl	100.00		55.00	95.00			

Inverted Chevron

	Blue	Green	White	Vaseline/ Canary	Cranberry	Other	
Vase	65.00	65.00	50.00				

Inverted Coindot

	Blue	Green	White	Vaseline/ Canary	Cranberry	Other	
Tumbler		60.00	35.00				
Rose Bowl			55.00	90.00			

Inverted Fan & Feather*

	Blue	Green	White	Vaseline/ Canary	Cranberry	Other	
Pitcher	750.00		600.00				
Tumbler	90.00		65.00				
Butter	500.00		390.00				
Sugar	300.00		235.00				
Creamer	225.00		165.00				
Spooner	225.00		165.00				
Rose Bowl		285.00*		150.00			
Bowl, Master	300.00	375.00		190.00			
Bowl, Sauce	85.00	90.00		40.00			
Cruet, rare	495.00						
Shakers, pair, rare	350.00						
Jelly Compote, rare	250.00		175.00				
Toothpick, rare	500.00						
Punchbowl, rare	650.00						
Punch Cup, rare	45.00						
Novelty Bowl, v. rare		250.00*		285.00*			
Spittoon Whimsey	350.00*		270.00*	340.00*			
Plate, very rare				500.00*			
Vase Whimsey, rare	200.00*	200.00*	150.00*				
Card Tray Whimsey	225.00	250.00	170.00	250.00			
Rose Bowl Whimsey, lg	250.00	265.00	210.00	250.00			

	Blue	Green	White	Vaseline/ Canary	Cranberry	Other
Iris With Meander						
Pitcher	390.00	375.00	285.00	320.00		
Tumbler	80.00	75.00	60.00	75.00		
Butter	295.00	275.00	220.00	275.00		
Sugar	160.00	145.00	90.00	160.00		
Creamer	95.00	80.00	65.00	75.00		
Spooner	95.00	80.00	60.00	80.00		
Bowl, Master	200.00	145.00	70.00	150.00		
Bowl, Sauce, 2 sizes	40.00 – 50.00	25.00 – 35.00	18.00 – 24.00	40.00		
Toothpick Holder	135.00	120.00	70.00	110.00		
Shakers, pair	210.00	200.00	165.00	190.00		
Cruet	465.00	395.00	275.00	395.00		450.00 Amber
Jelly Compote	55.00	50.00	35.00	45.00		
Vase, tall	60.00	55.00	40.00	60.00		
Pickle Dish	85.00	75.00	55.00	75.00		
Plate	90.00	85.00	65.00	80.00		
Jackson						
Pitcher	460.00		375.00	430.00		
Tumbler	80.00		65.00	80.00		
Butter	210.00		130.00	200.00		
Sugar	120.00		90.00	115.00		
Creamer	80.00		60.00	70.00		
Spooner	80.00		60.00	70.00		
Bowl, Master	85.00		70.00	75.00		
Bowl, Sauce	35.00		20.00	30.00		
Cruet	185.00		160.00	175.00		
Epergne, small	170.00		95.00	135.00		
Candy Dish	55.00		35.00	50.00		
Powder Jar	70.00		40.00	65.00		
Jazz						
Vase	50.00	55.00	35.00			
Jefferson #270						
Master Bowl	90.00	85.00	60.00			
Sauce	40.00	40.00	30.00			
Jefferson Shield						
Bowl, rare	250.00	300.00	175.00			
Jefferson Spool						
Vase	50.00	45.00	40.00			
Vase Whimsey	55.00	50.00	45.00			
Jefferson Stripe						
Vase, Jack-in-the-Pulpit	60.00	65.00	45.00			
Jefferson Wheel						
Bowl	55.00	50.00	40.00			
Jewel & Fan						
Bowl	60.00	55.00	45.00			
Banana Bowl	110.00	125.00	90.00			

	Blue	Green	White	Vaseline/ Canary	Cranberry	Other	
Jewel & Flower							
Pitcher	675.00		310.00	500.00			
Tumbler	90.00		65.00	80.00			
Butter	365.00		210.00	325.00			
Sugar	200.00		125.00	190.00			
Creamer	115.00		90.00	150.00			
Spooner	110.00		85.00	125.00			
Bowl, Master	70.00		50.00	70.00			
Bowl, Sauce	35.00		25.00	35.00			
Cruet	675.00		310.00	625.00			
Shakers, pair	160.00		105.00	150.00			
Novelty Bowl	50.00		30.00	50.00			
Jewelled Heart							
Pitcher	395.00	295.00	175.00				
Tumbler	80.00	65.00	40.00				
Butter	325.00	295.00	200.00				
Sugar	195.00	180.00	125.00				
Creamer	160.00	150.00	95.00				
Spooner	160.00	150.00	95.00				
Bowl, Master	65.00	60.00	50.00				
Bowl, Sauce	30.00	25.00	20.00				
Cruet	400.00	400.00	300.00				
Novelty Bowl	45.00	40.00	30.00				
Plate, small	70.00	65.00	50.00				
Compote	150.00	150.00	100.00				
Toothpick	250.00	230.00	190.00				
Sugar Shaker	350.00	325.00	275.00				
Syrup	500.00	475.00	395.00				
Shakers, pair	350.00	325.00	275.00				
Condiment Set (4 pieces, complete)	1,000.00	1,000.00	750.00				
Tray	250.00	225.00	175.00				
Jewels & Drapery							
Novelty Bowl	55.00	50.00	35.00			70.00	Aqua
Vase (from bowl)	50.00	45.00	30.00			75.00	Aqua
Jolly Bear							
Bowl	300.00	325.00	190.00				
Keyhole							
Bowl, scarce	85.00	90.00	65.00				
Keystone (Colonial)							
Compote, Hdld	75.00						
King Richard							
Compote	200.00		150.00	225.00			
Lady Caroline							
Creamer, 2 shapes	60.00			60.00			
Sugar, 2 shapes	56.00			55.00			
Basket	65.00			60.00			

	Blue	Green	White	Vaseline/ Canary	Cranberry	Other	
Whimsey, 3 handled	75.00			70.00			
Spill	65.00			65.00			
Lady Chippendale							
Compote, Tall						90.00	Cobalt
Late Coinspot							
Pitcher	150.00	140.00	110.00				
Tumbler	40.00	35.00	27.00				
Lattice & Daisy							
Tumbler, scarce	75.00		60.00	125.00			
Lattice & Points							
Hat Shape			60.00				
Vase			70.00				
Bowl, Novelty			55.00				
Lattice Medallions							
Bowl	55.00	50.00	45.00				
Laura (Single Flower Framed)							
Bowl, scarce	55.00	50.00	36.00				
Plate, ruffled, rare	150.00*	150.00*	125.00*				
Nappy, scarce	60.00	55.00	40.00				
Laurel Swag & Bows							
Shade (gas)						100.00	Amethyst
Leaf & Beads							
Bol, Ftd. or Dome	60.00	55.00	40.00				
Rose Bowl	75.00	70.00	50.00				
Bowl, Whimsey	70.00	60.00	45.00			95.00	Lime
Leaf & Diamonds							
Bowl	50.00		30.00				
Leaf & Leaflets (Long Leaf)							
Bowl	60.00		45.00				
Leaf Chalice							
Novelty compote	100.00	115.00	65.00	90.00		175.00	Cobalt
(found in several shapes from same mould							
Leaf Mold							
Pitcher					520.00		
Tumbler					100.00		
Butter					410.00		
Sugar					285.00		
Creamer					170.00		
Spooner					160.00		
Bowl, Master					130.00		
Bowl, Sauce					50.00		
Syrup					375.00		
Sugar Shaker					350.00		
Celery Vase					320.00		

	Blue	Green	White	Vaseline/ Canary	Cranberry	Other
Shakers, pair					550.00	
Cruet					630.00	
Toothpick Holder					475.00	
Leaf Rosette & Beads						
Bowl, scarce	250.00	260.00	200.00			
Lined Heart						
Vase	42.00	40.00	32.00			
Linking Rings						
Bowl	60.00					
Pitcher	120.00					
Juice Glass	40.00					
Compote	75.00					
Little Nell						
Vase	40.00	35.00	22.00			
Little Swan* (Pastel Swan)						
Novelty, 2 sizes	85.00	90.00	50.00	85.00		
Lords & Ladies						
Creamer	65.00			70.00		
Open Sugar	70.00			75.00		
Butter	90.00			100.00		
Plate, 7½"	100.00			110.00		
Lorna						
Vase	40.00		30.00	40.00		
Lustre Flute						
Pitcher	375.00		320.00			
Tumbler	95.00		60.00			
Butter	495.00		275.00			
Sugar	265.00		180.00			
Creamer	140.00		115.00			
Spooner	140.00		115.00			
Bowl, Master	275.00	320.00	220.00			
Bowl, Sauce	50.00		35.00			
Custard Cup	40.00		30.00			
Vase	60.00		47.00			
Many Loops						
Bowl	50.00	48.00	39.00			
Rose Bowl	75.00	70.00	50.00			
Many Ribs (Model Flint)						
Vase	40.00		30.00	40.00		
Maple Leaf						
Jelly Compote	110.00	100.00	70.00	200.00		
Maple Leaf Chalice						
One Shape	65.00	75.00	45.00	60.00		
Markham Swirl Band						
Oil Lamp	275.00		250.00	260.00	550.00	

	Blue	Green	White	Vaseline/ Canary	Cranberry	Other
Mary Ann						
Vase, rare	295.00		270.00			400.00 Amethyst
May Basket						
Basket Shape	80.00	75.00	60.00	95.00		
Meander						
Novelty Bowl	60.00	55.00	37.00			
Melon Optic Swirl						
Bowl, rare	80.00*	90.00*	60.00*	85.00*		
Melon Swirl						
Pitcher	450.00					
Tumbler	75.00					
Milky Way (Country Kitchen Vt.)						
Bowl, rare Millersburg			300.00*			
Plate, rare			400.00*			
Miniature Epergne						
Epergne, one lily	150.00			150.00		
Monkey (Under A Tree)						
Pitcher, rare			1,000.00*			
Tumbler, rare			500.00			
National Swirl						
Pitcher	275.00	260.00				
Tumbler	50.00	45.00				
Nesting Robin						
Bowl			290.00			
Netted Roses						
Bowl	70.00		50.00			
Plate	120.00		100.00			
Northern Star						
Bowl	65.00	60.00	45.00			
Plate	100.00	95.00	60.00			
Banana Bowl	75.00	70.00	50.00			
Northwood Block						
Novelty Bowl	50.00	45.00	30.00	45.00		
Celery Vase	60.00	60.00	40.00	55.00		
Northwood Stripe						
Vase	90.00	85.00	65.00	85.00		
Northwood's Many Ribs						
Vase	65.00	60.00	50.00	60.00		
Ocean Shell						
Novelty, Ftd., 3 variations	85.00	80.00	60.00			
Old Man Winter						
Basket, small	75.00	100.00	60.00			
Basket, large, Footed	150.00	175.00	95.00	275.00		

	Blue	Green	White	Vaseline/ Canary	Cranberry	Other
Opal Open* (Beaded Panels)						
Ring Bowl, Handled	90.00	85.00	60.00	85.00		
Bowl, Novelty	50.00	55.00	30.00	50.00		
Vase, Novelty	40.00	40.00	30.00	40.00		
Rose Bowl, Novelty	50.00	60.00	35.00	50.00		
Opal Spiral						
Sugar	350.00*					
Tumbler	90.00*					
Opal Urn						
Vase	75.00		50.00	80.00		
Open O's						
Bowl Novelty	50.00	45.00	30.00	45.00		
Spittoon Novelty	110.00	100.00	75.00	100.00		
Rose Bowl Novelty	90.00	85.00	60.00	85.00		
Optic Bastket						
One Shape				150.00		
Optic Panel						
Vase JIP				100.00		
Orange Tree						
Mug, rare						250.00* Custard Opal
Over-All Hob						
Pitcher	220.00		155.00	195.00		
Tumbler	60.00		30.00	50.00		
Butter	240.00		165.00	220.00		
Sugar	175.00		95.00	150.00		
Creamer	95.00		45.00	85.00		
Spooner	95.00		50.00	85.00		
Bowl, Master	75.00		35.00	65.00		
Bowl, Sauce	30.00		25.00	28.00		
Toothpick Holder	195.00		135.00	185.00		
Celery Vase	75.00		50.00	70.00		
Finger Bowl	55.00		35.00	55.00		
Mug	70.00		50.00	75.00		
Overlapping Leaves (Leaf Tiers)						
Bowl, Footed, lg	165.00	170.00	140.00			
Plate, Footed, lg	250.00	260.00	180.00			
Rose Bowl, Footed, lg	170.00	175.00	145.00			
Palisades						
Vase, Novelty	50.00	45.00	35.00	55.00		
Bowl, Novelty	45.00	50.00	35.00	50.00		
Palm & Scroll						
Bowl, Footed	65.00	60.00	40.00	60.00		
Rose Bowl, Footed	75.00	70.00	50.00	70.00		
Palm Beach						
Pitcher	450.00			470.00		
Tumbler	90.00			100.00		

	Blue	Green	White	Vaseline/ Canary	Cranberry	Other	
Butter	300.00			285.00			
Sugar	200.00			220.00			
Creamer	140.00			135.00			
Spooner	140.00			145.00			
Bowl, Master	85.00			80.00			
Bowl, Sauce, 2 sizes	40.00			45.00			
Jelly Compote	175.00		150.00	195.00			
Nappy, Handled, rare				425.00			
Plate, 8", rare	500.00			475.00			
Wine, very rare				400.00			
Plate, 10", rare	600.00			600.00			
Finger Bowl	250.00			250.00			
Panelled Flowers							
Rose Bowl, Footed	75.00		45.00				
Nut Cup, Footed	85.00		50.00				
Panelled Holly							
Pitcher	850.00		600.00				
Tumbler	125.00		90.00				
Butter	400.00		300.00				
Sugar	275.00		195.00				
Creamer	160.00		125.00				
Spooner	160.00		125.00				
Bowl, Master	195.00		135.00				
Bowl, Sauce	75.00		50.00				
Shakers, pair	260.00		170.00				
Novelty Bowl	85.00		60.00				
Panelled Sprig							
Cruet			135.00				
Toothpick Holder			95.00				
Shakers, pair			110.00				
Peacock Tail							
Tumbler, rare	85.00	90.00	70.00				
Peacocks (On the Fence)							
Bowl	275.00		150.00			350.00	Cobalt
Pearl Flowers							
Nut Bowl, Footed	50.00	45.00	35.00				
Novelty Bowl, Footed	60.00	50.00	30.00				
Rose Bowl, Footed	70.00	75.00	45.00				
Pearls & Scales							
Compote	65.00	60.00	40.00	75.00		80.00	Emerald
Rose Bowl, rare	90.00	95.00	55.00	90.00		100.00	Emerald
Piasa Bird							
Bowl	55.00		40.00				
Vase	70.00		60.00				
Rose Bowl	85.00		70.00				
Spittoon Whimsey	90.00		80.00				
Plate, Ftd.	110.00		95.00				

	Blue	Green	White	Vaseline/ Canary	Cranberry	Other
Picadilly						
Basket, small	90.00	85.00	70.00			
Pineapple & Fan						
Vase				400.00		
Pinecones & Leaves						
Bowl			70.00			
Plain Jane						
Nappy, Footed	50.00	60.00	35.00	85.00		
Plain Panels						
Vase	45.00	40.00	30.00			
Plume Panels Variant						
Vase, very rare	250.00	250.00	165.00			
Poinsettia						
Pitcher, either shape	350.00 – 500.00	375.00 – 550.00	250.00 – 400.00		750.00 – 1,300.00	
Tumbler	75.00		45.00		125.00	
Syrup, various	300.00 – 700.00	350.00 – 750.00	200.00 – 450.00		450.00 – 900.00	
Sugar Shaker	300.00	300.00	190.00		450.00	
Fruit Bowl	125.00	110.00	85.00		165.00	
Poinsettia Lattice **(Lattice & Poinsettia)**						
Bowl, scarce	435.00		275.00	650.00		
Polka Dot*						
Pitcher, rare	250.00		150.00		850.00	
Tumbler	70.00		35.00		110.00*	
Syrup	250.00		125.00		725.00*	
Sugar Shaker	195.00		145.00		295.00	
Toothpick Holder	425.00		295.00		525.00	
Shakers, pair	95.00		60.00		295.00*	
Cruet	395.00*		250.00*		750.00*	
Bowl, large	75.00		55.00		125.00	
Popsicle Sticks						
Bowl, Footed	55.00	50.00	40.00			
Pressed Coinspot **(#617 or Concave Columns)**						
Compote	65.00	75.00	50.00	70.00		
Card Tray	75.00	95.00	60.00	100.00		
Primrose (Daffodils Variant)						
Pitcher			900.00			
Prince Albert & Victoria						
Open Sugar	65.00		60.00			
Creamer, Footed	65.00		60.00			
Prince William						
Open Sugar	65.00			60.00		
Creamer	65.00			60.00		
Oval Plate	50.00			50.00		

	Blue	Green	White	Vaseline/ Canary	Cranberry	Other
Pitcher	100.00			100.00*		
Tumbler	40.00			37.00*		
Princess Diana						
Crimped Plate	65.00			60.00		
Butter	100.00			95.00		
Open Sugar	70.00			65.00		
Creamer	55.00			50.00		
Pitcher	125.00			115.00		
Tumbler	40.00			35.00		
Water Tray	55.00			50.00		
Bisquit Set (Jar & Plate, Complete)	90.00			95.00		
Salad Bowl	55.00			50.00		
Novelty Bowl	50.00			45.00		
Compote, metal base	145.00*			135.00		
Compote, large	85.00			90.00		
Oval Bowl	90.00			100.00		
Pulled Loop						
Vase, scarce, 2 sizes	40.00 – 80.00	55.00 – 90.00	30.00 – 60.00			
Pump & Trough*						
Pump	130.00		100.00	120.00		
Trough	75.00		50.00	60.00		
Queen's Crown						
Bowl, small	40.00					
Compote, low	60.00					
Question Mark*						
Compote	65.00	85.00	50.00	150.00		
Card Tray	75.00					
Quilted Daisy						
Fairy Lamp	500.00*		375.00*	450.00*		
Quilted Pillow Sham						
Oval Butter	100.00			90.00		
Creamer	70.00			65.00		
Open Sugar	70.00			60.00		
Ray						
Vase	55.00	50.00	35.00			
Rayed Heart						
Compote	65.00	60.00	50.00			
Rayed Jane						
Nappy	50.00		30.00			
Reflecting Diamonds						
Bowl	55.00	60.00	40.00			
Reflections						
Bowl	50.00	50.00	35.00			

	Blue	Green	White	Vaseline/ Canary	Cranberry	Other
Regal (Northwood's)						
Pitcher	300.00	285.00	190.00			
Tumbler	85.00	70.00	40.00			
Butter	225.00	175.00	125.00			
Sugar	135.00	90.00	70.00			
Creamer	100.00	60.00	50.00			
Spooner	90.00	60.00	50.00			
Bowl, Master	125.00	150.00	110.00			
Bowl, Sauce	35.00	40.00	20.00			
Cruet	800.00	800.00	700.00			
Shakers, pair	400.00	400.00	300.00			
Celery Vase	150.00	175.00	90.00			
Plate, rare	150.00	150.00	90.00			
Reverse Drapery						
Bowl	45.00	45.00	30.00			
Plate	90.00	85.00	55.00			
Vase	40.00	40.00	35.00			
Reverse Swirl						
Pitcher	250.00		175.00	220.00	795.00	
Tumbler	60.00		30.00	50.00	90.00	
Butter	195.00		135.00	165.00	250.00	
Sugar	170.00		110.00	150.00	220.00	
Creamer	120.00		90.00	110.00	185.00	
Spooner	120.00		85.00	95.00	145.00	
Bowl, Master	70.00		40.00	55.00	85.00	
Bowl, Sauce	25.00		20.00	25.00	40.00	
Cruet	265.00		110.00	170.00	465.00	
Toothpick Holder	155.00		95.00	125.00	265.00	
Sugar Shaker	170.00		115.00	140.00	270.00	
Syrup	175.00		100.00	140.00	425.00	
Mustard Pot	80.00		45.00	70.00	100.00	
Water Bottle	145.00		95.00	135.00	190.00	
Finger Bowl	70.00		45.00		100.00	
Shakers, pair	90.00		60.00	90.00	165.00	
Custard Cup	50.00		35.00		150.00	
Mini-Lamp	360.00		195.00		300.00	
Celery Vase	165.00		100.00	150.00	200.00	
Cruet Set and Holder, 4 pieces	295.00		200.00		365.00	
Oil Lamp	350.00		285.00	325.00		525.00
Hanging Lamp, rare					1,700.00*	
Rib & Big Thumprints						
Vase	45.00	40.00	30.00			
Ribbed Coinspot						
Pitcher, rare					1,050.00	
Tumbler, rare					170.00	
Syrup, rare					1,375.00	
Celery Vase, rare					295.00	
Creamer, rare					495.00	
Sugar Shaker					550.00	

	Blue	Green	White	Vaseline/Canary	Cranberry	Other
Ribbed Lattice						
Pitcher	275.00		220.00		975.00	
Tumbler	50.00		40.00		150.00	
Cruet	225.00		165.00		495.00	
Shakers, pair	130.00		90.00		295.00	
Syrup	175.00		140.00		600.00	
Butter	215.00		175.00		800.00	
Sugar	120.00		95.00		650.00	
Creamer	75.00		65.00		400.00	
Spooner	75.00		65.00		400.00	
Bowl, Master	70.00		45.00		140.00	
Bowl, Sauce	30.00		20.00		35.00	
Toothpick Holder	295.00		160.00		300.00	
Sugar Shaker, 2 sizes	140.00		90.00		410.00	
Ribbed Opal Rings						
Pitcher, rare					825.00	
Tumbler					115.00	
Ribbed Optic						
Tumble-up	70.00	80.00	50.00	75.00	90.00	
Ribbed Spiral						
Pitcher	500.00		365.00	465.00		
Tumbler	115.00		60.00	100.00		
Butter	375.00		295.00	350.00		
Sugar	200.00		150.00	175.00		
Creamer	95.00		45.00	65.00		
Spooner	110.00		55.00	75.00		
Bowl, Master	75.00		45.00	65.00		
Bowl, Sauce	30.00		20.00	26.00		
Plate	75.00		45.00	60.00		
Cup/Saucer set	110.00		60.00	90.00		
Toothpick Holder	175.00		135.00	165.00		
Shakers, pair	210.00		135.00	200.00		
Jelly Compote	70.00		50.00	65.00		
Bowl	55.00		40.00	50.00		
Vase, many sizes	40.00 – 90.00		30.00 – 60.00	40.00 – 80.00		
Whimsey, 3-handled				120.00*		
Richelieu						
Jelly Compote	75.00		55.00	70.00		
Bowl	70.00		50.00	65.00		
Creamer	65.00		45.00	60.00		
Open Sugar	65.00		45.00	60.00		
Divided Dish, rare	95.00		75.00	90.00		
Cracker Jar w/lid	195.00		165.00	185.00		
Basket, Handled	90.00		60.00	80.00		
Nappy, Handled	85.00		70.00	85.00		
Basket, open	100.00		70.00	90.00		
Pitcher	150.00		130.00	145.00		
Tumbler	25.00		20.00	25.00		
Tray	55.00		40.00	50.00		
Triple Sweet Dish	70.00		60.00	70.00		

	Blue	Green	White	Vaseline/ Canary	Cranberry	Other
Ric-Rac						
Jar				90.00		
Ring Handle						
Shakers, pair	100.00		70.00			
Ring Tray	100.00	90.00	70.00			
Ripple						
Vase	90.00	85.00	60.00	85.00		
Rippled Rib						
Vase			40.00			
Rococco						
Bowl, Bride's Basket	300.00		250.00	300.00	400.00	
Rose (Also called Rose & Ruffles)						
Candlestick, pair	250.00			250.00		
Cologne	250.00			250.00		
Vase, 6"	90.00			90.00		
Powder Jar (2 sizes)	125.00			125.00		
Pomade	100.00			100.00		
Covered Bowl (large)	150.00			150.00		
Tray, Dresser	90.00			90.00		
Pin Tray (or Soap Dish)	70.00			70.00		
Tall Compote	95.00			95.00		
Cosole Bowl	80.00			80.00		
Tray, Center handled	85.00			85.00		
Rose Show						
Bowl	275.00		190.00			
Rose Spatter						
Pitcher, rare						400.00 Tortoise shell
Rose Spray						
Compote	50.00	60.00	35.00			60.00 Amethyst
Roulette						
Novelty Bowl	50.00	45.00	35.00			
Plate	100.00	100.00	70.00			
Royal Scandal						
Wall Vase	250.00		200.00	250.00		
Rubina Verde						
Vase					290.00	
Ruffles & Rings						
Novelty Bowl	50.00	45.00	35.00			
Nut Bowl	55.00	50.00	40.00			
Rose Bowl	60.00	55.00	45.00			
Ruffles & Rings with Daisy Band						
Bowl, Footed	110.00	100.00	65.00			
S-Repeat						
Pitcher	500.00*		350.00*			
Tumbler	65.00		45.00			
Bowl, Master	85.00	95.00	70.00			115.00 Lime

	Blue	Green	White	Vaseline/Canary	Cranberry	Other	
Scheherezade							
Novelty Bowl	50.00	47.00	35.00				
Scottish Moor							
Pitcher	350.00		275.00		475.00	400.00	Rubina
Tumbler	80.00		65.00		100.00	95.00	Amethyst
Cruet	395.00		225.00				
Cracker Jar	350.00		210.00				
Celery Vase	150.00		95.00				
Scroll With Acanthus							
Pitcher	395.00		350.00	350.00			
Tumbler	90.00		75.00	75.00			
Butter	370.00		350.00	350.00			
Sugar	170.00		150.00	135.00			
Creamer	90.00		70.00	75.00			
Spooner	85.00		75.00	70.00			
Bowl, Master	55.00		40.00	50.00			
Bowl, Sauce	25.00		20.00	25.00			
Jelly Compote	65.00		60.00	60.00			
Toothpick Holder	285.00		275.00	310.00			
Cruet	225.00		220.00	375.00			
Shakers, pair	210.00		195.00	200.00			
Sea Scroll							
Compote	150.00	145.00	100.00				
Seafoam							
Compote	275.00		200.00				
Seaspray							
Nappy	47.00	45.00	37.00				
Whimsey	50.00	50.00	40.00				
Seweed							
Pitcher	350.00		250.00		425.00		
Tumbler	65.00		40.00		110.00		
Butter	200.00		120.00		395.00		
Sugar	165.00		135.00		210.00		
Creamer	125.00		95.00		200.00		
Spooner	125.00		90.00		175.00		
Bowl, Master	60.00		40.00		125.00		
Bowl, Sauce	30.00		20.00		70.00		
Cruet, 2 shapes	250.00		140.00		695.00		
Syrup	175.00		135.00		525.00		
Sugar Shaker	215.00		170.00		425.00		
Toothpick Holder	325.00		235.00		500.00		
Celery Vase	100.00		80.00		175.00		
Shakers, pair	150.00		110.00		350.00		
Pickle Castor, complete					500.00		
Rose Bowl			500.00*				
Shell & Dots							
Rose Bowl	47.00		35.00				
Novelty Bowl	52.00		40.00	95.00			
Nut Bowl	45.00		40.00				
Shell & Wild Rose							
Novelty Bowl, Open-edge	60.00	55.00	45.00	100.00			

	Blue	Green	White	Vaseline/ Canary	Cranberry	Other
Shell, Beaded*						
Pitcher	560.00	625.00	495.00			
Tumbler	90.00	115.00	75.00			
Butter	500.00	675.00	425.00			
Sugar	225.00	260.00	185.00			
Creamer	150.00	180.00	145.00			
Spooner	150.00	180.00	145.00			
Bowl, Master	85.00	100.00	70.00			
Bowl, Sauce	55.00	65.00	40.00			
Cruet	500.00	695.00	400.00			
Toothpick Holder	475.00	675.00	500.00			
Shakers, pair	350.00	400.00	295.00			
Condiment set, 4 pc.	800.00	900.00	700.00			
Jelly Compote, very rare	900.00*	900.00*	700.00*	900.00*		
Simple Simon						
Compote	65.00	60.00	45.00			
Singing Birds						
Mug, rare	350.00		300.00*	600.00*		
Tumbler Whimsey, very rare	1,500.00					
Single Lily Spool						
Epergne	195.00	190.00	170.00	250.00		
Single Poinsettia						
Bowl			275.00			
Sir Lancelot						
Bowl, Footed	67.00	65.00	45.00			
Smooth Rib						
Bowl				35.00		
Snowflake						
Night Lamp	1,300.00*		795.00*		1,795.00	
Hand Lamp	395.00*		275.00*		600.00	
Oil Lamp	325.00*		220.00*		550.00	
Somerset						
Pitcher, Juice, 5½"	60.00		50.00			
Tumbler, 3"	30.00		26.00			
Oval Dish, 9"	45.00		37.00			
Square Dish	50.00		45.00			
Sowerby Salt						
Salt Dish	65.00	70.00	60.00			
Spanish Lace*						
Pitcher	250.00 – 500.00		110.00 – 300.00	220.00 – 450.00	650.00 – 1,000.00	
Tumbler	60.00		40.00	55.00	110.00	
Butter	410.00		220.00	395.00	500.00	
Sugar	260.00		195.00	250.00	320.00	
Spooner	140.00		90.00	130.00	175.00	
Creamer	140.00		90.00	125.00	175.00	
Bowl, Master	90.00		65.00	80.00	150.00	
Bowl, Sauce	30.00		25.00	30.00	40.00	

	Blue	Green	White	Vaseline/ Canary	Cranberry	Other	
Syrup	250.00		175.00	350.00	650.00		
Sugar Shaker	150.00		100.00	140.00	200.00		
Celery Vase	120.00		85.00	135.00	175.00		
Shakers, pair	110.00		75.00	115.00	220.00		
Finger Bowl	70.00		55.00	85.00	150.00		
Bride's Basket, 2 sizes	125.00		90.00	140.00	200.00		
Jam Jar	290.00		195.00	325.00	500.00		
Cracker Jar	700.00				900.00		
Perfume Bottle	190.00		100.00	215.00	270.00		
Mini-Lamp	200.00		130.00	210.00	350.00		
Water Bottle	300.00		195.00	320.00	425.00		
Vase, many sizes	95.00		50.00	105.00	210.00		
Rose Bowl, many sizes	75.00		50.00	70.00	140.00		
Cruet	275.00		195.00	295.00	750.00		
Liquer Jug					850.00		
Spatter							
Vase, 9"	95.00	90.00	60.00	90.00			
Bowl	55.00	50.00	35.00	50.00	110.00		
Pitcher	250.00	245.00	185.00	240.00	450.00		
Tumbler	30.00	30.00	20.00	30.00	75.00		
Spattered Coinspot							
Pitcher					450.00		
Tumbler					90.00		
Spokes & Wheels							
Bowl	55.00	50.00	37.00				
Plate, rare	85.00	80.00				125.00	Aqua
Spool							
Compote	45.00	45.00	35.00				
Spool of Threads							
Compote	60.00		40.00	50.00			
Squirrel & Acorn							
Vase	90.00	80.00	75.00				
Bowl	85.00	75.00	70.00				
Compote	90.00	80.00	75.00				
Whimsey	90.00	85.00	75.00				
Stag & Holly							
Bowl, Footed, rare			2,000.00*			1,500.00	Amethyst
Star Base							
Square Bowl	40.00						
Stars & Bars							
Pull Knob, each			15.00				
Stars & Stripes*							
Pitcher			240.00		1,100.00		
Tumbler	100.00		70.00				
Lamp Shade			65.00				
Barber Bottle			100.00		295.00		

	Blue	Green	White	Vaseline/ Canary	Cranberry	Other
Compote, age uncertain					375.00	
Stork & Rushes						
Mug	95.00		175.00			
Tumbler			60.00			
Stork & Swan						
Syrup			150.00			
Strawberry						
Bon-Bon			220.00*			
Bowl						100.00 Amethyst
Stripe*						
Pitcher	275.00				560.00	
Tumbler	55.00				90.00	
Syrup	275.00				450.00	
Toothpick Holder	250.00				395.00	
Condiment Set	395.00				750.00*	
Barber Bottle	160.00				295.00	
Shakers, pair	100.00				250.00	
Rose Bowl	90.00				200.00	
Oil Lamp					600.00	
Bowl			60.00		100.00	
Vase			60.00		120.00	
Cruet					500.00 – 750.00	
Stripe, Wide						
Pitcher	250.00		160.00		450.00	
Tumbler	60.00		40.00		100.00	
Syrup	220.00		180.00		325.00	
Sugar Shaker	175.00		150.00		260.00	
Cruet	195.00	500.00	160.00		550.00	
Toothpick Holder	265.00	400.00	210.00		350.00	
Shakers, pair			140.00		240.00	
Shade	75.00					
Sunburst On Shield (Diadem)						
Pitcher	600.00			950.00		
Tumbler	125.00			200.00		
Bowl, Master	140.00			195.00		
Bowl, Sauce	35.00			40.00		
Breakfast Set, 2 pieces	185.00			250.00		
Nappy, rare	220.00			340.00		
Cruet, rare	325.00		350.00	750.00		
Butter	375.00		250.00	395.00		
Sugar	225.00		175.00	250.00		
Creamer	140.00		95.00	135.00		
Spooner	140.00		95.00	135.00		
Novelty Bowl 7½"	90.00		70.00	95.00		

	Blue	Green	White	Vaseline/ Canary	Cranberry	Other
Sunk Honeycomb						
Bowl, very rare				200.00*		
Surf Spray						
Pickle Dish	60.00	55.00	40.00			
Swag With Brackets						
Pitcher	295.00	280.00	195.00	275.00		
Tumbler	85.00	75.00	45.00	75.00		
Butter	265.00	250.00	195.00	250.00		
Sugar	140.00	135.00	75.00	130.00		
Creamer	95.00	85.00	55.00	80.00		
Spooner	95.00	110.00	55.00	100.00		
Bowl, Master	75.00	65.00	45.00	65.00		
Bowl, Sauce	35.00	35.00	25.00	30.00		
Toothpick Holder	350.00	295.00	240.00	290.00		
Shakers, pair	195.00	175.00	130.00	180.00		
Cruet	500.00	320.00	170.00	240.00		
Jelly Compote	60.00	55.00	35.00	50.00		
Bowl	50.00	45.00	30.00	45.00		
Whimsey Sugar	160.00*			160.00*		
Swastika						
Pitcher	900.00	900.00	675.00		1,100.00*	
Tumbler	100.00	125.00	80.00		150.00	
Syrup	950.00	950.00	850.00		1,300.00	
Swirl						
Pitcher, various	125.00 – 200.00	110.00 – 190.00	60.00 – 110.00	295.00	250.00 – 650.00	
Tumbler	30.00	27.00	16.00	45.00	95.00	
Butter	125.00	120.00	70.00		155.00	
Sugar	90.00	95.00	50.00		160.00	
Creamer	70.00	80.00	40.00		95.00	
Spooner	70.00	80.00	40.00		125.00	
Bowl, Master	50.00	55.00	45.00		75.00	
Bowl, Sauce	20.00	25.00	16.00		36.00	
Syrup	115.00	110.00	75.00		155.00	
Sugar Shaker	135.00	100.00	70.00		165.00	
Cruet, 2 sizes	165.00	195.00	100.00		285.00	
Shakers, pair	170.00	150.00	100.00		240.00	
Fingerbowl	65.00	60.00	37.00		95.00	
Toothpick Holder	110.00	120.00	70.00		145.00	
Mustard Jar	95.00	100.00	58.00		145.00	
Rose Bowl	60.00	70.00	40.00		90.00	
Celery Vase	75.00	85.00	55.00		140.00	
Custard Cup	40.00	50.00	30.00		75.00	
Water, Bitters & Bar						
Bottles, each	90.00 – 250.00	90.00 – 195.00	65.00 – 100.00		350.00 – 450.00	
Lampshade	100.00	90.00	40.00		175.00	
Cheese Dish			240.00		395.00	
Fingerlamp			350.00		600.00	
Cruet Set, complete					475.00	

	Blue	Green	White	Vaseline/ Canary	Cranberry	Other
Strawholder, rare	800.00		575.00		1,150.00	
Vase	60.00	65.00	37.00		150.00	
Shot Glass	80.00		65.00			
Swirling Maze						
Pitcher, any, (avg.)	475.00	450.00	300.00		795.00	
Tumbler	60.00	55.00	30.00		95.00	
Salad Bowl	95.00	90.00	60.00		145.00	
Target						
Vase	110.00	110.00	90.00			
Thistle Patch						
Novelty, Footed			40.00			
Thousand Eye						
Pitcher			90.00			
Tumbler			25.00			
Butter			125.00			
Sugar			90.00			
Creamer			75.00			
Spooner			75.00			
Celery Vase			90.00			
Cruet			140.00			
Shakers, pair			70.00			
Toothpick Holder			120.0			
Bottles, various			25.00 – 50.00			
Bowl, various			25.00 – 45.00			
Compote, various			40.00 – 75.00			
Thread & Rib						
Epergne	800.00	900.00	600.00	800.00		
Epergne Whimsey	850.00	950.00	650.00	850.00		
Threaded Grape						
Large Compote, 8"	150.00	165.00	95.00			
Three Fingers & Panel						
Bowl, Master, rare	95.00		70.00	95.00		
Bowl, Sauce, rare	35.00		25.00	35.00		
Three Fruits						
Bowl, scarce	200.00		125.00			
Three Fruits with Meander						
Bowl, Footed	175.00		110.00			
Tines						
Vase		75.00				
Tiny Tears						
Vase	50.00	45.00	35.00			
Tokyo*						
Pitcher	350.00	300.00	160.00			
Tumbler	75.00	70.00	45.00			
Butter	185.00	175.00	85.00			
Sugar	140.00	130.00	60.00			

	Blue	Green	White	Vaseline/Canary	Cranberry	Other
Creamer	90.00	80.00	40.00			
Spooner	90.00	85.00	45.00			
Vase	55.00	50.00	35.00			
Cruet	185.00	180.00	90.00			
Syrup	150.00	145.00	70.00			
Jelly Compote	55.00	55.00	30.00			
Plate	70.00	70.00	35.00			
Bowl, Master	45.00	40.00	25.00			
Bowl, Sauce	30.00	30.00	15.00			
Shakers, pair	90.00	85.00	45.00			
Toothpick Holder	250.00	200.00	125.00			
Trailing Vine						
Novelty Bowl	60.00		40.00	55.00		
Tree of Life						
Vase	100.00		60.00			
Shakers, each	100.00		50.00			
Tree of Love						
Novelty Bowl			40.00			
Compote			50.00			
Plate, rare, 2 sizes			135.00*			
Covered Butter, rare			350.00			
Tree Stump						
Mug	90.00	100.00	60.00			
Tree Trunk						
Vase	40.00	45.00	30.00			
Trellis						
Tumbler				65.00		
Triangle						
Matchholder	75.00		55.00			
Trout						
Bowl			150.00*			
Twig						
Vase, small, 5½"	65.00	75.00	50.00	70.00		
Vase, Panelled, 7"	85.00	90.00	65.00	80.00		
Vase Whimsey	95.00	100.00	80.00	70.00		
Twist (miniatures)						
Butter	270.00		170.00	260.00		
Sugar	140.00		80.00	130.00		
Creamer	85.00		45.00	80.00		
Spooner	85.00		50.00	80.00		
Twisted Ribs						
Vase	45.00	40.00	30.00			

	Blue	Green	White	Vaseline/ Canary	Cranberry	Other	
Twister							
Bowl	50.00	45.00	35.00				
Plate	95.00						
Vase, whimsey	65.00	70.00	45.00				
Venetian Optic							
Lamp (mini night lamp)	125.00*		95.00		300.00*		
Venetian (Spider Web)							
Vase	75.00						
Venice							
Oil Lamp	385.00		340.00				
Victoria & Albert							
Covered Butter	150.00		110.00	140.00			
Sugar	85.00		60.00	75.00			
Creamer	75.00		50.00	70.00			
Bisquit Jar	150.00		110.00	140.00			
Victorian							
Vase, applied flowers and vine	150.00	165.00	110.00	155.00		175.00	Amber
Victorian Hamper							
Handled Basket	75.00			70.00			
Vintage, Northwood/Dugan							
Bowl	45.00	50.00	30.00				
Rose Bowl	55.00	60.00	35.00				
Plate	70.00	75.00	50.				
Vintage Leaf, Fenton							
Bowl, rare	150.00						
Vulcan							
Creamer	60.00*		50.00*				
Sugar	75.00*		65.00*				
Spooner	60.00*		50.00*				
Butter	120.00*		110.00*				
Waffle							
Epergne						750.00	Olive
War Of The Roses							
Bowl	70.00			65.00			
Boat Shape, lg	120.00			120.00			
Boat Shade, sm	100.00			100.00			
Compote, metal stand	150.00			140.00			
Waterlily & Cattails (Fenton)							
Pitcher	420.00	395.00	250.00			425.00	Amethyst
Tumbler	70.00	60.00	30.00			80.00	Amethyst
Butter	395.00	350.00	240.00			410.00	Amethyst
Sugar	200.00	150.00	100.00			220.00	Amethyst
Creamer	100.00	75.00	60.00			110.00	Amethyst
Spooner	100.00	75.00	60.00			115.00	Amethyst
Bowl, Master	70.00	65.00	50.00			75.00	Amethyst
Bowl, Sauce	35.00	30.00	25.00			35.00	Amethyst

	Blue	Green	White	Vaseline/Canary	Cranberry	Other	
Novelty Bowl	45.00	40.00	30.00			55.00	Amethyst
Bon-Bon	70.00	65.00	45.00			80.00	Amethyst
Relish, Handled	95.00	90.00	70.00			120.00	Amethyst
Plate	90.00	85.00	60.00			100.00	Amethyst
Breakfast Set, 2 pcs.	145.00	135.00	100.00			165.00	Amethyst
Gravy Boat, Handled	60.00	55.00	40.00			75.00	Amethyst
Rose Bowl	75.00		50.00			125.00	Amethyst

Waterlily & Cattails (Northwood)

	Blue	Green	White	Vaseline/Canary	Cranberry	Other	
Tumbler, rare	100.00						

Wheel & Block

	Blue	Green	White	Vaseline/Canary	Cranberry	Other	
Novelty Bowl	45.00	40.00	30.00				
Vase Whimsey	55.00	45.00	35.00				
Novelty Plate	125.00	95.00	65.00				

Wide Panel

	Blue	Green	White	Vaseline/Canary	Cranberry	Other	
Epergne, 4 Lily	800.00	850.00	600.00	900.00 rare			

Wide Rib

	Blue	Green	White	Vaseline/Canary	Cranberry	Other	
Vase	60.00	70.00	50.00				

Wild Bouquet

	Blue	Green	White	Vaseline/Canary	Cranberry	Other	
Pitcher	275.00	240.00	190.00				
Tumbler	120.00	100.00	40.00				
Butter	495.00	450.00	325.00				
Sugar	295.00	260.00	185.00				
Creamer	195.00	150.00	100.00				
Spooner	195.00	150.00	100.00				
Bowl, Master	195.00	165.00	95.00				
Bowl, Sauce	60.00	50.00	40.00				
Cruet	395.00	425.00	250.00				
Toothpick Holder	425.00	375.00	225.00				
Shakers, pair	180.00	170.00	125.00				
Cruet Set w/tray	475.00	425.00	300.00				
Jelly Compote	160.00	130.00	90.00				

Wild Daffodils

	Blue	Green	White	Vaseline/Canary	Cranberry	Other	
Mug	80.00		60.00			95.00	Amethyst
						150.00	Custard Opal

Wild Rose

	Blue	Green	White	Vaseline/Canary	Cranberry	Other	
Bowl	60.00		40.00			70.00	Amethyst
Banana Bowl	70.00		50.00			80.00	Amethyst
Stemmed Sherbet	65.00		55.00			70.00	Amethyst

William & Mary

	Blue	Green	White	Vaseline/Canary	Cranberry	Other	
Creamer	65.00			60.00			
Open Sugar, stemmed	70.00			65.00			
Master Salt	50.00						
Compote	95.00			90.00			
Cake Plate, stemmed	140.00			130.00			
Plate	100.00			95.00			
Covered Butterdish	195.00			185.00			

	Blue	Green	White	Vaseline/ Canary	Cranberry	Other
Wilted Flowers						
Bowl	50.00	60.00	40.00			
Handled Basket	95.00	100.00	60.00			
Windflower						
Bowl, rare	165.00		120.00			
Nappy, rare			275.00			
Windows (Plain)*						
Pitcher, various	130.00 – 190.00		85.00 – 135.00		350.00 – 550.00	
Tumbler	55.00		35.00		110.00	
Mini Lamp	165.00				1,800.00	
Fingerbowl	50.00		47.00		75.00	
Oil Lamp					600.00	
Shade	60.00		35.00		195.00	
Barber Bottle					325.00	
Toothpick Holder					325.00	
Windows (Swirled)						
Pitcher, various	300.00 – 400.00		200.00 – 300.00		600.00 – 800.00	
Tumbler	85.00		65.00		120.00	
Butter	400.00		300.00		550.00	
Sugar	250.00		170.00		350.00	
Creamer	90.00		70.00		225.00	
Spooner	90.00		70.00		225.00	
Bowl, Master	55.00		40.00		95.00	
Bowl, Sauce	30.00		25.00		55.00	
Toothpick Holder	300.00		175.00		375.00	
Mustard Jar	75.00		55.00		150.00	
Cruet	310.00		220.00		475.00	
Sugar Shaker	150.00		110.00		325.00	
Syrup, 2 shapes	295.00		195.00		500.00	
Shakers, pair	165.00		120.00		295.00	
Cruet Set, complete	265.00		195.00		600.00	
Celery Vase	90.00		50.00		165.00	
Plate, 2 sizes	110.00		65.00		250.00	
Barber Bottle						
Windsor Stripe						
Vase					120.00	
Winged Scroll						
Nappy, rare				150.00		
Winter Cabbage						
Bowl, Footed	47.00	45.00	36.00			
Winterlily						
Vase	100.00	95.00	50.00			100.00 Lime
Wishbone & Drapery						
Bowl	47.00	42.00	36.00			
Plate	60.00	57.00	50.00			

	Blue	Green	White	Vaseline/Canary	Cranberry	Other
Woven Wonder						
Rose Bowl	60.00		40.00			
Novelty Bowl	55.00		38.00			
Wreath & Shell						
Pitcher	595.00		195.00	365.00		
Tumbler, Flat or Footed	110.00		50.00	70.00		
Butter	250.00		135.00	210.00		
Sugar	200.00		95.00	150.00		
Creamer	160.00		80.00	130.00		
Spooner	160.00		80.00	120.00		
Bowl, Master	95.00		70.00	110.00		
Bowl, Sauce	37.00		25.00	32.00		
Celery Vase	180.00		100.00	160.00		
Rose Bowl	95.00		65.00	80.00		
Toothpick Holder	295.00		195.00	265.00		
Ladies Spittoon	95.00		65.00	115.00		
Cracker Jar	595.00		460.00	540.00		
Salt Dip	130.00		85.00	95.00		
Novelty Bowl	70.00	150.00	55.00	65.00		
Ivy Ball, rare	165.00		120.00	150.00		
(from flat tumbler mould)						

Note: Add 10% for decorated items.

	Blue	Green	White	Vaseline/Canary	Cranberry	Other
Wreathed Cherry*						
Butter	85.00					
Creamer	70.00					
Sugar	75.00					
Spooner	60.00					

Note: Age questionable on all pieces.

	Blue	Green	White	Vaseline/Canary	Cranberry	Other
Venetian Optic						
Venetian Optic Lamp (Mini Night Lamp)	125.00*		95.00		300.00*	
Zipper & Loops						
Vase, Footed	60.00	65.00	47.00			

Standard Encyclopedia of CARNIVAL GLASS, 5th Edition

by Bill Edwards

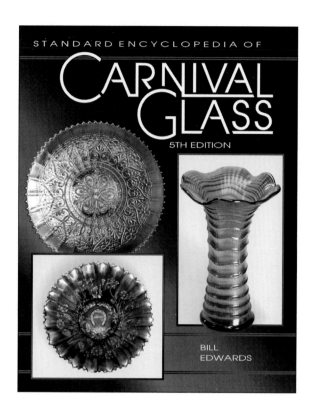

The new 5th edition of the *Standard Encyclopedia of Carnival Glass* is so completely revised — you won't recognize it! Remarkably, it introduces 80 new patterns and many never before printed photos. It also has been beautifully redesigned to better meet the reader's needs. This comprehensive reference is loaded with nearly 1,000 patterns, all photographed in full color and described in detail with important facts, histories, and sizes. The illustrated price guide also has many, many additions. It includes virtually every piece of carnival glass ever made — well over 7,000 pieces. It is bound within the encyclopedia but is also offered separately and can be used independently. A multitude of American and foreign companies are represented here, such as Dugan, Fenton, Imperial, Millersburg, Northwood, Cambridge, Jenkins, Westmoreland, Fostoria, Heisey, McKee-Jeanette, and the U.S. Glass Company. This 5th edition is the finest one yet and will continue to hold the respect and trust of glass collectors worldwide.
ISBN: 0-89145-689-9 • #4634 • 8½ x 11 • 352 Pgs. • HB • **$24.95**

Standard Encyclopedia of Carnival Glass Price Guide, 10th Edition.
ISBN: 0-89145-689-9 • **#4635** • 8½ x 11 • 64 Pgs. • PB • **$9.95**

COLLECTOR BOOKS
Informing Today's Collector

For over two decades we have been keeping collectors informed on trends and values in all fields of antiques and collectibles.

DOLLS, FIGURES & TEDDY BEARS

4707	A Decade of **Barbie** Dolls & Collectibles, 1981–1991, Summers	$19.95
4631	**Barbie** Doll Boom, 1986–1995, Augustyniak	$18.95
2079	**Barbie** Doll Fashions, Volume I, Eames	$24.95
3957	**Barbie** Exclusives, Rana	$18.95
4632	**Barbie** Exclusives, Book II, Rana	$18.95
4557	**Barbie**, The First 30 Years, Deutsch	$24.95
4657	**Barbie** Years, 1959–1995, Olds	$16.95
3310	**Black Dolls**, 1820–1991, Perkins	$17.95
3873	**Black Dolls**, Book II, Perkins	$17.95
1529	Collector's Encyclopedia of **Barbie** Dolls, DeWein	$19.95
4506	Collector's Guide to **Dolls in Uniform**, Bourgeois	$18.95
3727	Collector's Guide to **Ideal Dolls**, Izen	$18.95
3728	Collector's Guide to Miniature **Teddy Bears**, Powell	$17.95
3967	Collector's Guide to **Trolls**, Peterson	$19.95
4571	**Liddle Kiddles**, Identification & Value Guide, Langford	$18.95
4645	**Madame Alexander** Dolls Price Guide #21, Smith	$9.95
3733	**Modern Collector's** Dolls, Sixth Series, Smith	$24.95
3991	**Modern Collector's** Dolls, Seventh Series, Smith	$24.95
4647	**Modern Collector's** Dolls, Eighth Series, Smith	$24.95
4640	Patricia Smith's **Doll Values**, Antique to Modern, 12th Edition	$12.95
3826	Story of **Barbie**, Westenhouser	$19.95
1513	**Teddy Bears & Steiff** Animals, Mandel	$9.95
1817	**Teddy Bears & Steiff** Animals, 2nd Series, Mandel	$19.95
2084	**Teddy Bears, Annalee's & Steiff** Animals, 3rd Series, Mandel	$19.95
1808	Wonder of **Barbie**, Manos	$9.95
1430	World of **Barbie** Dolls, Manos	$9.95

FURNITURE

1457	American **Oak** Furniture, McNerney	$9.95
3716	American **Oak** Furniture, Book II, McNerney	$12.95
1118	Antique **Oak** Furniture, Hill	$7.95
2132	Collector's Encyclopedia of **American** Furniture, Vol. I, Swedberg	$24.95
2271	Collector's Encyclopedia of **American** Furniture, Vol. II, Swedberg	$24.95
3720	Collector's Encyclopedia of **American** Furniture, Vol. III, Swedberg	$24.95
3878	Collector's Guide to **Oak** Furniture, George	$12.95
1755	Furniture of the **Depression Era**, Swedberg	$19.95
3906	**Heywood-Wakefield** Modern Furniture, Rouland	$18.95
1885	**Victorian** Furniture, Our American Heritage, McNerney	$9.95
3829	**Victorian** Furniture, Our American Heritage, Book II, McNerney	$9.95
3869	**Victorian** Furniture books, 2 volume set, McNerney	$19.90

JEWELRY, HATPINS, WATCHES & PURSES

1712	Antique & Collector's **Thimbles** & Accessories, Mathis	$19.95
1748	Antique **Purses**, Revised Second Ed., Holiner	$19.95
1278	Art Nouveau & Art Deco **Jewelry**, Baker	$9.95
4558	**Christmas Pins**, Past and Present, Gallina	$18.95
3875	Collecting Antique **Stickpins**, Kerins	$16.95
3722	Collector's Ency. of **Compacts, Carryalls & Face Powder Boxes**, Mueller	$24.95
4655	Complete Price Guide to **Watches**, #16, Shugart	$26.95
1716	Fifty Years of Collectible **Fashion Jewelry**, 1925–1975, Baker	$19.95
1424	**Hatpins** & Hatpin Holders, Baker	$9.95
4570	Ladies' **Compacts**, Gerson	$24.95
1181	100 Years of Collectible **Jewelry**, 1850–1950, Baker	$9.95
2348	20th Century Fashionable Plastic **Jewelry**, Baker	$19.95
3830	Vintage **Vanity Bags & Purses**, Gerson	$24.95

TOYS, MARBLES & CHRISTMAS COLLECTIBLES

3427	**Advertising Character** Collectibles, Dotz	$17.95
2333	Antique & Collector's **Marbles**, 3rd Ed., Grist	$9.95
3827	Antique & Collector's **Toys**, 1870–1950, Longest	$24.95
3956	Baby Boomer **Games**, Identification & Value Guide, Polizzi	$24.95
3717	**Christmas** Collectibles, 2nd Edition, Whitmyer	$24.95
1752	**Christmas** Ornaments, Lights & Decorations, Johnson	$19.95
4649	Classic Plastic **Model Kits**, Polizzi	$24.95

4559	Collectible **Action Figures**, 2nd Ed., Manos	$17.95
3874	Collectible **Coca-Cola Toy Trucks**, deCourtivron	$24.95
2338	Collector's Encyclopedia of **Disneyana**, Longest, Stern	$24.95
4639	Collector's Guide to **Diecast Toys & Scale Models**, Johnson	$19.95
4651	Collector's Guide to **Tinker Toys**, Strange	$18.95
4566	Collector's Guide to **Tootsietoys**, 2nd Ed., Richter	$19.95
3436	**Grist's** Big Book of **Marbles**	$19.95
3970	**Grist's** Machine-Made & Contemporary **Marbles**, 2nd Ed.	$9.95
4569	**Howdy Doody**, Collector's Reference and Trivia Guide, Koch	$16.95
4723	**Matchbox®** Toys, 1948 to 1993, Johnson, 2nd Ed.	$18.95
3823	**Mego** Toys, An Illustrated Value Guide, Chrouch	15.95
1540	**Modern Toys** 1930–1980, Baker	$19.95
3888	**Motorcycle** Toys, Antique & Contemporary, Gentry/Downs	$18.95
4728	**Schroeder's** Collectible **Toys**, Antique to Modern Price Guide, 3rd Ed.	$17.95
1886	**Stern's** Guide to **Disney** Collectibles	$14.95
2139	**Stern's** Guide to **Disney** Collectibles, 2nd Series	$14.95
3975	**Stern's** Guide to **Disney** Collectibles, 3rd Series	$18.95
2028	**Toys**, Antique & Collectible, Longest	$14.95
3979	**Zany Characters** of the Ad World, Lamphier	$16.95

INDIANS, GUNS, KNIVES, TOOLS, PRIMITIVES

1868	Antique **Tools**, Our American Heritage, McNerney	$9.95
2015	Archaic **Indian** Points & Knives, Edler	$14.95
1426	**Arrowheads** & Projectile Points, Hothem	$7.95
4633	**Big Little Books**, Jacobs	$18.95
2279	**Indian** Artifacts of the Midwest, Hothem	$14.95
3885	**Indian** Artifacts of the Midwest, Book II, Hothem	$16.95
1964	**Indian** Axes & Related Stone Artifacts, Hothem	$14.95
2023	**Keen Kutter** Collectibles, Heuring	$14.95
4724	**Modern Guns**, Identification & Values, 11th Ed., Quertermous	$12.95
4505	Standard Guide to **Razors**, Ritchie & Stewart	$9.95
4730	Standard **Knife** Collector's Guide, 3rd Ed., Ritchie & Stewart	$12.95

PAPER COLLECTIBLES & BOOKS

4633	**Big Little Books**, Jacobs	$18.95
1441	Collector's Guide to **Post Cards**, Wood	$9.95
2081	Guide to Collecting **Cookbooks**, Allen	$14.95
4648	**Huxford's** Old Book Value Guide, 8th Ed.	$19.95
2080	Price Guide to **Cookbooks** & Recipe Leaflets, Dickinson	$9.95
2346	**Sheet Music** Reference & Price Guide, 2nd Ed., Pafik & Guiheen	$18.95
4654	**Victorian Trading Cards**, Historical Reference & Value Guide, Cheadle	$19.95

GLASSWARE

1006	**Cambridge Glass** Reprint 1930–1934	$14.95
1007	**Cambridge Glass** Reprint 1949–1953	$14.95
4561	Collectible **Drinking Glasses**, Chase & Kelly	$17.95
4642	Collectible **Glass Shoes**, Wheatley	$19.95
4553	Coll. **Glassware** from the 40's, 50's & 60's, 3rd Ed., Florence	$19.95
2352	Collector's Encyclopedia of **Akro Agate Glassware**, Florence	$14.95
1810	Collector's Encyclopedia of **American Art Glass**, Shuman	$29.95
3312	Collector's Encyclopedia of **Children's Dishes**, Whitmyer	$19.95
4552	Collector's Encyclopedia of **Depression Glass**, 12th Ed., Florence	$19.95
1664	Collector's Encyclopedia of **Heisey Glass**, 1925–1938, Bredehoft	$24.95
3905	Collector's Encyclopedia of **Milk Glass**, Newbound	$24.95
1523	Colors In **Cambridge Glass**, National Cambridge Society	$19.95
4564	**Crackle Glass**, Weitman	$19.95
2275	**Czechoslovakian Glass** and Collectibles, Barta/Rose	$16.95
4714	**Czechoslovakian Glass** and Collectibles, Book II, Barta/Rose	$16.95
4716	**Elegant Glassware** of the Depression Era, 7th Ed., Florence	$19.95
1380	Encylopedia of **Pattern Glass**, McClain	$12.95
3981	**Ever's** Standard **Cut Glass** Value Guide	$12.95
4659	**Fenton Art Glass**, 1907–1939, Whitmyer	$24.95
3725	**Fostoria**, Pressed, Blown & Hand Molded Shapes, Kerr	$24.95
3883	**Fostoria Stemware**, The Crystal for America, Long & Seate	$24.95
3318	**Glass Animals** of the Depression Era, Garmon & Spencer	$19.95
4644	**Imperial Carnival Glass**, Burns	$18.95

COLLECTOR BOOKS
Informing Today's Collector

3886	**Kitchen Glassware** of the Depression Years, 5th Ed., Florence	$19.95
2394	**Oil Lamps II**, Glass Kerosene Lamps, Thuro	$24.95
4725	Pocket Guide to **Depression Glass**, 10th Ed., Florence	$9.95
4634	Standard Encyclopedia of **Carnival Glass**, 5th Ed., Edwards	$24.95
4635	Standard **Carnival Glass** Price Guide, 10th Ed.	$9.95
3974	Standard Encyclopedia of **Opalescent Glass**, Edwards	$19.95
4731	**Stemware Identification**, Featuring Cordials with Values, Florence	$24.95
3326	**Very Rare Glassware** of the Depression Years, 3rd Series, Florence	$24.95
3909	**Very Rare Glassware** of the Depression Years, 4th Series, Florence	$24.95
4732	**Very Rare Glassware** of the Depression Years, 5th Series, Florence	$24.95
4656	**Westmoreland Glass**, Wilson	$24.95
2224	World of **Salt Shakers**, 2nd Ed., Lechner	$24.95

POTTERY

4630	**American Limoges**, Limoges	$24.95
1312	**Blue & White Stoneware**, McNerney	$9.95
1958	So. Potteries **Blue Ridge Dinnerware**, 3rd Ed., Newbound	$14.95
1959	**Blue Willow**, 2nd Ed., Gaston	$14.95
3816	Collectible **Vernon Kilns**, Nelson	$24.95
3311	Collecting **Yellow Ware** – Id. & Value Guide, McAllister	$16.95
1373	Collector's Encyclopedia of **American Dinnerware**, Cunningham	$24.95
3815	Collector's Encyclopedia of **Blue Ridge Dinnerware**, Newbound	$19.95
4658	Collector's Encyclopedia of **Brush-McCoy Pottery**, Huxford	$24.95
2272	Collector's Encyclopedia of **California Pottery**, Chipman	$24.95
3811	Collector's Encyclopedia of **Colorado Pottery**, Carlton	$24.95
2133	Collector's Encyclopedia of **Cookie Jars**, Roerig	$24.95
3723	Collector's Encyclopedia of **Cookie Jars**, Volume II, Roerig	$24.95
3429	Collector's Encyclopedia of **Cowan Pottery**, Saloff	$24.95
4638	Collector's Encyclopedia of **Dakota Potteries**, Dommel	$24.95
2209	Collector's Encyclopedia of **Fiesta**, 7th Ed., Huxford	$19.95
4718	Collector's Encyclopedia of **Figural Planters & Vases**, Newbound	$19.95
3961	Collector's Encyclopedia of **Early Noritake**, Alden	$24.95
1439	Collector's Encyclopedia of **Flow Blue China**, Gaston	$19.95
3812	Collector's Encyclopedia of **Flow Blue China**, 2nd Ed., Gaston	$24.95
3813	Collector's Encyclopedia of **Hall China**, 2nd Ed., Whitmyer	$24.95
3431	Collector's Encyclopedia of **Homer Laughlin China**, Jasper	$24.95
1276	Collector's Encyclopedia of **Hull Pottery**, Roberts	$19.95
4573	Collector's Encyclopedia of **Knowles, Taylor & Knowles**, Gaston	$24.95
3962	Collector's Encyclopedia of **Lefton China**, DeLozier	$19.95
2210	Collector's Encyclopedia of **Limoges Porcelain**, 2nd Ed., Gaston	$24.95
2334	Collector's Encyclopedia of **Majolica Pottery**, Katz-Marks	$19.95
1358	Collector's Encyclopedia of **McCoy Pottery**, Huxford	$19.95
3963	Collector's Encyclopedia of **Metlox Potteries**, Gibbs Jr.	$24.95
3313	Collector's Encyclopedia of **Niloak**, Gifford	$19.95
3837	Collector's Encyclopedia of **Nippon Porcelain I**, Van Patten	$24.95
2089	Collector's Ency. of **Nippon Porcelain**, 2nd Series, Van Patten	$24.95
1665	Collector's Ency. of **Nippon Porcelain**, 3rd Series, Van Patten	$24.95
3836	**Nippon Porcelain** Price Guide, Van Patten	$9.95
1447	Collector's Encyclopedia of **Noritake**, Van Patten	$19.95
3432	Collector's Encyclopedia of **Noritake**, 2nd Series, Van Patten	$24.95
1037	Collector's Encyclopedia of **Occupied Japan**, Vol. I, Florence	$14.95
1038	Collector's Encyclopedia of **Occupied Japan**, Vol. II, Florence	$14.95
2088	Collector's Encyclopedia of **Occupied Japan**, Vol. III, Florence	$14.95
2019	Collector's Encyclopedia of **Occupied Japan**, Vol. IV, Florence	$14.95
2335	Collector's Encyclopedia of **Occupied Japan**, Vol. V, Florence	$14.95
3964	Collector's Encyclopedia of **Pickard China**, Reed	$24.95
1311	Collector's Encyclopedia of **R.S. Prussia**, 1st Series, Gaston	$24.95
1715	Collector's Encyclopedia of **R.S. Prussia**, 2nd Series, Gaston	$24.95
3726	Collector's Encyclopedia of **R.S. Prussia**, 3rd Series, Gaston	$24.95
3877	Collector's Encyclopedia of **R.S. Prussia**, 4th Series, Gaston	$24.95
1034	Collector's Encyclopedia of **Roseville Pottery**, Huxford	$19.95
1035	Collector's Encyclopedia of **Roseville Pottery**, 2nd Ed., Huxford	$19.95
3357	**Roseville** Price Guide No. 10	$9.95
3965	Collector's Encyclopedia of **Sascha Brastoff**, Conti, Bethany & Seay	$24.95
3314	Collector's Encyclopedia of **Van Briggle** Art Pottery, Sasicki	$24.95
4563	Collector's Encyclopedia of **Wall Pockets**, Newbound	$19.95
2111	Collector's Encyclopedia of **Weller Pottery**, Huxford	$29.95
3452	Coll. Guide to **Country Stoneware & Pottery**, Raycraft	$11.95
2077	Coll. Guide to **Country Stoneware & Pottery**, 2nd Series, Raycraft	$14.95
3434	Coll. Guide to **Hull Pottery**, The Dinnerware Line, Gick-Burke	$16.95

3876	Collector's Guide to **Lu-Ray Pastels**, Meehan	$18.95
3814	Collector's Guide to **Made in Japan** Ceramics, White	$18.95
4646	Collector's Guide to **Made in Japan** Ceramics, Book II, White	$18.95
4565	Collector's Guide to **Rockingham**, The Enduring Ware, Brewer	$14.95
2339	Collector's Guide to **Shawnee Pottery**, Vanderbilt	$19.95
1425	**Cookie Jars**, Westfall	$9.95
3440	**Cookie Jars**, Book II, Westfall	$19.95
3435	Debolt's Dictionary of **American Pottery Marks**	$17.95
2379	Lehner's Ency. of **U.S. Marks** on Pottery, Porcelain & China	$24.95
4722	**McCoy Pottery**, Collector's Reference & Value Guide, Hanson/Nissen	$19.95
3825	**Puritan Pottery**, Morris	$24.95
4726	**Red Wing Art Pottery**, 1920s–1960s, Dollen	$19.95
1670	**Red Wing Collectibles**, DePasquale	$9.95
1440	**Red Wing Stoneware**, DePasquale	$9.95
3738	**Shawnee Pottery**, Mangus	$24.95
4629	Turn of the Century **American Dinnerware**, 1880s–1920s, Jasper	$24.95
4572	**Wall Pockets** of the Past, Perkins	$17.95
3327	**Watt Pottery** – Identification & Value Guide, Morris	$19.95

OTHER COLLECTIBLES

4704	Antique & Collectible **Buttons**, Wisniewski	$19.95
2269	Antique **Brass & Copper** Collectibles, Gaston	$16.95
1880	Antique **Iron**, McNerney	$9.95
3872	Antique **Tins**, Dodge	$24.95
1714	**Black** Collectibles, Gibbs	$19.95
1128	**Bottle** Pricing Guide, 3rd Ed., Cleveland	$7.95
4636	**Celluloid Collectibles**, Dunn	$14.95
3959	**Cereal Box** Bonanza, The 1950's, Bruce	$19.95
3718	Collectible **Aluminum**, Grist	$16.95
3445	Collectible **Cats**, An Identification & Value Guide, Fyke	$18.95
4560	Collectible **Cats**, An Identification & Value Guide, Book II, Fyke	$19.95
1634	Collector's Ency. of Figural & Novelty **Salt & Pepper Shakers**, Davern	$19.95
2020	Collector's Ency. of Figural & Novelty **Salt & Pepper Shakers**, Vol. II, Davern	$19.95
2018	Collector's Encyclopedia of **Granite Ware**, Greguire	$24.95
3430	Collector's Encyclopedia of **Granite Ware**, Book II, Greguire	$24.95
4705	Collector's Guide to **Antique Radios**, 4th Ed., Bunis	$18.95
1916	Collector's Guide to **Art Deco**, Gaston	$14.95
3880	Collector's Guide to **Cigarette Lighters**, Flanagan	$17.95
4637	Collector's Guide to **Cigarette Lighters**, Book II, Flanagan	$17.95
1537	Collector's Guide to **Country Baskets**, Raycraft	$9.95
3966	Collector's Guide to **Inkwells**, Identification & Values, Badders	$18.95
3881	Collector's Guide to **Novelty Radios**, Bunis/Breed	$18.95
4652	Collector's Guide to **Transistor Radios**, 2nd Ed., Bunis	$16.95
4653	Collector's Guide to **TV Memorabilia**, 1960s–1970s, Davis/Morgan	$24.95
2276	**Decoys**, Kangas	$24.95
1629	**Doorstops**, Identification & Values, Bertoia	$9.95
4567	Figural **Napkin Rings**, Gottschalk & Whitson	$18.95
3968	**Fishing Lure** Collectibles, Murphy/Edmisten	$24.95
3817	**Flea Market Trader**, 10th Ed., Huxford	$12.95
3976	Foremost Guide to **Uncle Sam** Collectibles, Czulewicz	$24.95
4641	**Garage Sale & Flea Market Annual**, 4th Ed.	$19.95
3819	**General Store Collectibles**, Wilson	$24.95
4643	**Great American West** Collectibles, Wilson	$24.95
2215	Goldstein's **Coca-Cola** Collectibles	$16.95
3884	Huxford's Collectible **Advertising**, 2nd Ed.	$24.95
2216	**Kitchen Antiques**, 1790–1940, McNerney	$14.95
3321	Ornamental & Figural **Nutcrackers**, Rittenhouse	$16.95
2026	**Railroad** Collectibles, 4th Ed., Baker	$14.95
1632	**Salt & Pepper Shakers**, Guarnaccia	$9.95
1888	**Salt & Pepper Shakers** II, Identification & Value Guide, Book II, Guarnaccia	$14.95
2220	**Salt & Pepper Shakers** III, Guarnaccia	$14.95
3443	**Salt & Pepper Shakers** IV, Guarnaccia	$18.95
4555	**Schroeder's Antiques** Price Guide, 14th Ed., Huxford	$12.95
2096	**Silverplated Flatware**, Revised 4th Edition, Hagan	$14.95
1922	Standard **Old Bottle** Price Guide, Sellari	$14.95
4708	Summers' Guide to **Coca-Cola**	$19.95
3892	**Toy & Miniature Sewing Machines**, Thomas	$18.95
3828	Value Guide to **Advertising Memorabilia**, Summers	$18.95
3977	Value Guide to **Gas Station** Memorabilia, Summers & Priddy	$24.95
3444	**Wanted to Buy**, 5th Edition	$9.95

This is only a partial listing of the books on antiques that are available from Collector Books. All books are well illustrated and contain current values. Most of these books are available from your local bookseller, antique dealer, or public library. If you are unable to locate certain titles in your area, you may order by mail from COLLECTOR BOOKS, P.O. Box 3009, Paducah, KY 42002-3009. Customers with Visa or MasterCard may phone in orders from 7:00–4:00 CST, Monday–Friday, Toll Free 1-800-626-5420. Add $2.00 for postage for the first book ordered and $0.30 for each additional book. Include item number, title, and price when ordering. Allow 14 to 21 days for delivery.

Schroeder's
ANTIQUES
Price Guide

. . . is the #1 best-selling antiques & collectibles value guide on the market today, and here's why . . .

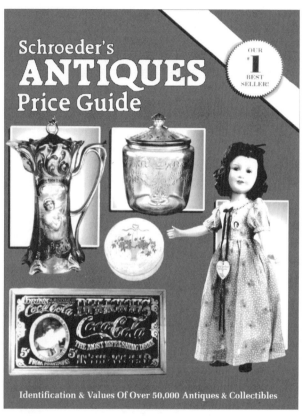

Schroeder's
ANTIQUES
Price Guide

OUR
#1
BEST
SELLER!

Identification & Values Of Over 50,000 Antiques & Collectibles

8½ x 11, 608 Pages, $12.95

• *More than 300 advisors, well-known dealers, and top-notch collectors work together with our editors to bring you accurate information regarding pricing and identification.*

• *More than 45,000 items in almost 500 categories are listed along with hundreds of sharp original photos that illustrate not only the rare and unusual, but the common, popular collectibles as well.*

• *Each large close-up shot shows important details clearly. Every subject is represented with histories and background information, a feature not found in any of our competitors' publications.*

• *Our editors keep abreast of newly developing trends, often adding several new categories a year as the need arises.*

If it merits the interest of today's collector, you'll find it in *Schroeder's*. And you can feel confident that the information we publish is up to date and accurate. Our advisors thoroughly check each category to spot inconsistencies, listings that may not be entirely reflective of market dealings, and lines too vague to be of merit. Only the best of the lot remains for publication.

Without doubt, you'll find
SCHROEDER'S ANTIQUES PRICE GUIDE
the only one to buy for
reliable information and values.

COLLECTOR BOOKS
A Division of Schroeder Publishing Co., Inc.